SOUP'S ON!

Cover art: *Cream of Squash Soup* © Edoneil, courtesy iStockphoto.com.

Cover design copyright © 2012 by Covenant Communications, Inc.
Cover and book design by Jennie Williams.

Published by Covenant Communications, Inc.
American Fork, Utah

Printed in China
First Printing: October 2012

19 18 17 16 15 14 13 12   10 9 8 7 6 5 4 3 2 1

ISBN-13: 978-1-62108-129-6

SOUP'S ON!

100 Savory Soups, Stews, and Chilies Made Easy

by VALERIE PHILLIPS

Covenant Communications, Inc.

TABLE OF CONTENTS

Introduction i

Using This Book.................................. iii

Shortcut Ingredients............................. v

Poultry Soups 1

Beef and Pork Soups 41

Seafood Soups 73

Vegetable Soups................................93

Bean and Nut Soups.........................139

Fruit and Cheese Soups.....................159

Tips for Savvy Soup-Makers...............172

SECTION 1: POULTRY SOUPS

Hearty Chicken Noodle Soup 2

Slow Cooker Chicken and Chives Stew................4

Turkey and Wild Rice Soup 5

Salsa Chicken Soup.......................................6

Old-Fashioned Chicken Vegetable Soup 8

Thai-Style Chicken Soup 10

Chicken Gnocchi Soup 12

Cilantro Lime Rice and Chicken Soup 13

Chipotle White Chicken Chili.............................14

Chicken Cacciatore (Hunter's Stew) 16

Cheddar Chicken and Broccoli Soup 18

Chicken Fajita Soup with Lime 20

Turkey Pot Pie Soup.....................................22

Easy Homemade Turkey Broth 23

Post-Thanksgiving Turkey Chili.........................24

Chicken Potato Florentine 26

Slow Cooker Nacho Chicken Soup.....................28

Avgolemono—Greek Egg Lemon Soup 30

Mulligatawny..32

Quick Creamy Chicken Noodle Soup..................33

Quick Chicken Tortilla Soup with Avocado 34

Chicken Paprikás..36

Slow Cooker Homemade Chicken Broth 38

SECTION 2: BEEF AND PORK SOUPS

Slow-Cooked Beef Stew over Rice.....................42

Beef Mushroom and Barley Stew.......................43

Beefy Vegetable and Noodle Soup.....................44

Beef and Biscuits 46

Terrific Taco Soup 48

RJ's Stuffed Pepper Soup 49

Rootin' Tootin' Cincinnati Chili..............50

Smoky Pork Chili Verde 52

Pasta and Ground Beef Soup 54

Italian Wedding Soup.............................55

Quick Tailgate Chili 56

Old-Fashioned Vegetable Beef Soup....................58

Beef Stroganoff Soup 60

Root Beer-Braised Beef Stew 61

Slow Cooker Smoky No-Bean Chili 62

Pepperoni Soupreme.............................64

Savory Sausage Tortellini Soup 66

Presto Zuppa Toscana 67

Beef Borscht 68

Hungarian Goulash 70

SECTION 3: SEAFOOD SOUPS

Bratten's Clam Chowder 74

Larry H. Miller's Seafood Gumbo 76

Golden Corn and Crab Chowder....................78

Rah-Rah! Ramen 79

Lobster Bisque 80

New Orleans Gumbo 82

Salmon Chowder.................................84

Kung Pao Shrimp Bowl........................86

Manhattan Clam Chowder 87

Thai-Style Curry Shrimp Soup 88

Cioppino 90

SECTION 4: VEGETABLE SOUPS

Broccoli Cheddar Soup 94

Loaded Potato Soup 96

Creamy Tomato Tortellini Soup 98

Minestrone 100

Minted Pea Soup..............................101

Biggest Loser Resort's Roasted Red Pepper Bisque. 102

Maple-Kissed Butternut Squash Bisque..............104

Creamy Cauliflower Soup 106

Cheesy Veggie Chowder...................108

Quick Vegetarian Veggie Soup..........110

Curried Carrot Bisque 111

Cream of Asparagus Soup 112

Fennel Bisque 114

French Onion Soup with Parmesan Croutons.....116

Zucchini and Bacon Soup 118

Gazpacho...119

Garden Tomato Bisque.......................120

Harvest Pumpkin Soup with Cheddar 122

Mega-Mushroom Soup 124

Roasted Garlic Bisque 126

Garden Vegetable Soup 128

Easy Cheesy Potato-Broccoli Soup 129

Silken Potato Leek Soup 130

Rosemary Potato and Corn Chowder 132

Rich Mushroom and Brown Rice Soup 134

Hotel Utah Borscht 136

Tangy Strawberry Soup 165

Tex-Mex Queso Soup 166

Better Cheddar Soup................................168

Cheesy Onion Soup 170

SECTION 5: BEAN AND NUT SOUPS

Slow Cooker Split Pea and Ham Soup...............140

West African-Style Peanut Soup.....................141

Thai-Style Peanut and Noodle Soup 142

Red Beans and Rice Soup 144

Tuscan Bean and Kale Soup 145

Chickpea and Spinach Soup.........................146

Spicy Black Bean Soup..............................148

Crunchy Almond-Celery Soup 149

Herbed Bean and Bacon Soup 150

Spicy Lentil and Sausage Stew......................152

Slow Cooker Vegetarian Lentil Stew 154

Black Bean and Ham Soup 155

Fifteen-Bean Soup 156

SECTION 6: FRUIT AND CHEESE SOUPS

Tropical Pineapple and Sweet Potato 160

Creamy Pear, Blue Cheese, and Bacon Soup 162

Watermelon Gazpacho 164

INTRODUCTION

Soup is the ultimate comfort food. Why?

There are so many different soups! They can be hot and spicy, chunky like stews and chili, or creamy and velvety smooth.

Soup can be a budget booster. You can stretch a handful of ingredients to feed a crowd, and it's a great way to use leftover vegetables and meats.

A basic soup recipe is the springboard for creativity. Season it to your taste, switch out one veggie for another, or bulk it up with rice, potatoes, or pasta.

It's a great way to enjoy good-for-you veggies. Those who shun a full serving of carrots or tomatoes

may not mind bits and pieces of them mingled in a savory broth.

Most soups allow leeway with cooking times. Late for dinner? Just keep it warm on the back burner or in a slow cooker.

Soup helps get your family around the table enjoying a meal together. Whether it's chili, vegetable beef, chicken noodle, or any other great soup, the welcoming aroma is a magnet.

And yet, the term "homemade soup" is intimidating, conjuring up the image of an all-day foray of making from-scratch stock, peeling and chopping vegetables, and slow simmering meats.

There's still hope for a harried weeknight, however. Here are one hundred soups that have been streamlined with shortcuts such as jarred salsa, frozen vegetables, and refrigerated beef tips. You can ladle out a hot and healthy dinner in the time it takes for pizza delivery to arrive.

These soups combine fresh ingredients with items that are likely already sitting in your pantry or spice rack. Simple garnishes such as croutons, chopped herbs, or a swirl of cream can further elevate your soup to better-than-convenience status. Many of the recipes can be made in thirty minutes. Some are designed to "make it fast; cook it slow," with a few minutes of assembly time and then a few hours in the oven or slow cooker.

Some folks may balk at the idea of using ready-cooked bacon or a packaged rice mix. In a perfect world, we would all be eating freshly cooked, from-scratch meals. But, in many families, there are nights when conflicting schedules allow a short window of opportunity where everyone's home at the same time. On those busy nights, you can spend less time in the kitchen and more time enjoying dinner together.

Even *New York Times* cooking guru Mark Bittman has said, "Cooking is compromise, after all. We almost never have the time, the ideal ingredients or equipment, or all of the skills we'd like."

Some soups actually benefit from a shorter cooking time. The pasta or rice has a firmer texture, and the veggies have brighter colors and flavor. If you've ever had restaurant broccoli soup that's been simmering too long, you'll agree that gray, mushy broccoli is unappetizing.

Some of these recipes, such as Tailgate Chili, Salmon Chowder, and Root Beer-Braised Beef Stew are hearty one-pot dinners. Others, such Curried Carrot Bisque, Cream of Asparagus Soup, and Tangy Strawberry Soup make an interesting starter course. And many of the soups can be paired with a sandwich or salad for a satisfying meal.

Soup's on!

USING THIS BOOK

Gather ingredients first. Take a few minutes to read through your recipe and gather all ingredients and equipment before you begin cooking. You'll waste valuable time if you realize halfway through the recipe that you really don't have a can of beans sitting in your pantry or that someone ate half the cheese you intended to use.

Combine cooking tasks. Wherever possible, I've tried to use just one pan rather than dirty several. For instance, tortellini soup recipes always have you boil the tortellini in water then drain it and add it to a soup. Why not just cook the tortellini in the soup to begin with?

Take advantage of simmer time. Most recipes in other cookbooks assume that you will prep all the meats and peel and chop all the veggies before you even turn on the stove. This adds precious minutes to your total cook time. Why not start your long-cooking ingredients simmering on the stove first; then, while you're waiting, chop or shred some of the short-cooking ingredients? In the following recipes, I've tried to capitalize on any waiting time by sandwiching tasks in between.

Preheating. Many of my recipes call for warming the cooking oil over low heat while you prep other ingredients then turning up the heat when you're ready to sauté. It saves a few minutes of heating time. Be sure to use low heat for safety; if you take more time chopping vegetables

than planned, or if you get distracted, burning oil could start a fire.

Cutting up. Most of these recipes were intended to keep prep work to a minimum. But there are times when peeling, slicing, and chopping can't be avoided. These tasks are easier with a good-quality cutting board that fits in the dishwasher for easy cleanup, a good, sharp chef's or Santoku knife, and a paring knife. If you'd rather use one of those handy-dandy chopping gadgets sold in infomercials, fine. But it takes me more time to assemble the parts then disassemble and clean them (and hope you don't lose any of the critical pieces) than it does to use a knife.

Puree pointers. Many soups are pureed for a smooth texture. If you have an immersion blender, you can do this right in the soup pot. Tip the pot to one side to collect the soup and make sure the blades of the blender are fully immersed before turning it on, otherwise you'll have flying soup. If you're using a stand blender, fill it only one-half to two-thirds full so there's ample room for any backsplash. If the soup is really hot, I like to leave the middle hole open to prevent steam buildup. (I once had a blender of pumpkin soup shoot out like a geyser when I hit the on button.) Experts at America's Test Kitchen advise a different technique: close the middle hole and hold the lid firmly in place with a kitchen towel. To minimize backsplash (or the geyser explosion mentioned above), start on the lowest speed for a minute before switching to high.

Storing. Most soups can be made ahead and frozen. I like to freeze any leftovers in single-size portions so they can be taken to work and microwaved for lunch. Flavors and textures may change with freezing. When you reheat the soup, taste it and adjust seasonings. Soups with pasta or rice may absorb much of the broth and turn mushy. Creamy soups may separate during thawing and will need stirring to blend everything back together.

Cutting fat. You can cut down on some of the fat in soups or broths by chilling it in the refrigerator then skimming off the fat that rises to the top and hardens. Many of my recipes use cream and butter, but others rely more on pureed, cooked vegetables or cornstarch as low-fat thickeners. I experimented with fat-free half-and-half and found that in many cases, it worked as well as regular. You can use milk or skim milk, but the broth will be thinner. Low-fat cream cheese or sour cream also works, but the fat-free versions don't offer the right flavor or texture.

SHORTCUT INGREDIENTS

Here are some frequently used shortcut ingredients you'll encounter in this book:

Canned or packaged broth or stock. Homemade chicken broth is usually better (depending on the cook's skills). But if you've got a half hour to get dinner on the table, skip the boiling carcasses. There are two easy recipes in this book for making chicken broth from your spent rotisserie chicken, and turkey stock from your Thanksgiving leftovers. You can portion and freeze it for later use. Just remember to label each container so you don't have to guess what you're thawing.

What's the difference between stock and broth? Stock is made mostly with bones and bits of meat trimmings. Broth is made with pieces of actual meat, so it's richer. But the terms are often interchangeable.

I also tested most of these recipes using chicken and beef bouillon cubes dissolved in water. These were a tad salty and contain MSG and lots of other suspicious-sounding ingredients, but they make a decent-tasting soup if you're on a budget.

Is there a difference in commercial broths? America's Test Kitchen, which does blind taste-testing of ingredients, gives high marks to Swanson's Certified Organic Free Range Chicken Broth, Swanson's Natural Goodness Chicken Broth, Swanson's Vegetarian Vegetable Broth, and Rachael Ray Stock-in-a-Box Beef Broth. When I first open a can or package, I like to be hit with a chicken-y aroma, and Swanson's broth also seems to have more flavor. When I open generic broths, I can't smell anything. But generic broth is usually about half the cost of Swanson's, and organic broth is more costly, so consider your budget.

Frozen mirepoix blend. Many soup recipes start out with a flavor base of aromatic vegetables—sautéed onion, celery, and carrots. In French cooking, this is called mirepoix (meer-pwah).

To avoid peeling and chopping, I often use a twelve-ounce package of frozen "mirepoix-style blend" of chopped onion, celery, and carrots, available in the frozen vegetable aisle of many supermarkets. It's also called "soup starter." The usual ratio is about 50 percent onion, 25 percent carrots, and 25 percent celery. If a recipe calls for a twelve-ounce bag of mirepoix blend and it's not available, chop up two-thirds cup onion, one-third cup celery, and one-third cup carrots for a close substitution.

Frozen vegetables. They are already prepped and will keep nicely in the freezer if you don't get around to using them right away. Supermarkets offer a wide variety of mixed veggies. I avoided using blends in most of my recipes because some vegetables take longer to cook than others. By the time the carrots are tender, the peas are overcooked and mushy. My recipes include specific times to add certain vegetables, depending on their cooking times. But if you want to be creative, go ahead and add different veggie blends to your soups. I've found that frozen vegetables have more volume because their moisture expands upon freezing. So it takes about one and a half cups of frozen chopped onion to equal one cup of fresh.

I've also found that frozen onions don't caramelize much when you sauté them due to the liquid from thawing. Some of my soups, such as French Onion Soup, Cheesy Onion Soup, and Garden Vegetable Soup, specify using fresh onions despite the trouble of peeling and slicing them, because the caramelization adds a layer of flavor.

Dried chopped onion. Onions add flavor and aroma to soups and so many other savory dishes. Dehydrated onions (also known as onion flakes or dried, minced onion) save a lot of time weeping over a cutting board. Their long shelf life makes them a great item for your pantry or long-term food storage. According to the seasonings company McCormick, one-fourth cup of dried onion equals one cup fresh chopped onion. They may not reconstitute to full size, but I believe they do add the same amount of flavor. Add them to soups at the beginning of the cooking process to give them time to reconstitute.

Legendary cook Julia Child said, "It's hard to imagine civilization without onions." With dried onions always ready on your pantry shelf, you won't have to.

Good-quality garlic powder. There are recipes where fresh garlic is critical, such as my Roasted Garlic Parmesan Bisque. But most of the time the garlic is a flavor agent and not the major ingredient. You'll save a lot of time peeling and mincing with a sprinkle of garlic powder. Don't use garlic salt or garlic powder with partially hydrogenated oil mixed into it. You can use jarred minced garlic, although it's more expensive. According to equivalency charts, a clove of garlic equals one teaspoon minced fresh garlic or one-eighth teaspoon garlic powder. But I personally don't think garlic powder has that much flavor strength, and I tend to use more. If you are making substitutions, let your own taste be your guide.

Packaged bacon bits. Bacon adds that smoky, salty flavor, but frying it is messy and time-consuming. Shelf-stable jarred or packaged real bacon pieces are already cooked and can sit in your pantry for a while. They have half the fat of home-fried bacon—and unfortunately, with that fat goes some of the flavor. But you also lose the calories. I prefer using the bagged bacon bits; the jarred ones seem to be more tough with less flavor.

Cream cheese. A lot of soups call for heavy cream, which you may not always have on hand. Cream cheese keeps for weeks in the refrigerator, it evenly disperses and thickens soups without curdling, and it adds a velvety tang as well. I've used the reduced-fat (Neufchatel) cream cheese with success; it just takes a little more time to blend. But don't use fat-free cream cheese; it doesn't melt into the soup and it has an off taste.

Velveeta. Velveeta has a bad rep as the ultimate in processed foods. Maybe you'll feel better knowing that some time-honored Tex-Mex restaurants in Texas use it for items like queso and cheese enchiladas because of its meltability, according to *Houston Press* food writer Robb Walsh. "Sure that first trip to the checkout counter with the screaming yellow Velveeta box in your shopping cart is going to be embarrassing. But you know it's the only way to summon up the déjà vu flavor of old-fashioned Tex-Mex at home."

That meltability is why I use Velveeta in three of my soup recipes—for creamy, cheesy flavor without risk of the soup curdling or going grainy.

Diced frozen hash browns and hash browns O'Brien. You can bypass peeling and dicing raw potatoes and chopping onion and green pepper. These frozen hash browns already have the onion and pepper bits mixed in. The diced type (not shredded) are a perfect size for vegetable or potato soups. They are also relatively inexpensive.

Canned tomatoes. Tomatoes add flavor and nutrition to soups. That includes V-8 juice, and tomato sauce or paste, depending on how much tomato presence you want. I love petite-diced canned tomatoes. The mini chunks are just the right size to float in soups. If it's fresh tomato season, you are welcome to use them instead. But canned tomatoes are so convenient. Some of my soups call for a small amount of tomato paste because it's high in umami, giving soups a savory, pleasant, full taste.

Salsa. With salsa, you don't have to deal with roasting and peeling chiles or dicing tomatoes or onions. (Notice how much I want to get out of chopping onions?) Salsa is low in fat and adds a bright flavor to soups. It's easy to adjust the heat level of your soup simply by using mild, medium, or hot salsa.

A close cousin is canned tomatoes with chiles. The Ro-Tel brand is the only one I'm familiar with. For testing purposes, I used mild salsa and the original Ro-Tel flavor.

Canned beans. Canned beans are ready when you are. For substitution purposes, one fifteen-ounce can contains about one and one-third cups of beans after they're drained and rinsed. Can weights can vary a few ounces with the type of beans and the brand.

Dried beans, per cooked serving, are usually less than half the price of canned beans. But you have to allow soaking time. You can let your slow cooker do the soaking. Place two cups of dry beans (black, white, navy, kidney, pinto) in the pot, and fill the pot about three-fourths of the way full with cold water. Put the lid on and set it on low for six to eight hours.

Rinse the beans well and use them as you would canned. Portion leftover beans to freeze for later use.

Rice mixes. The seasonings add layers of flavor to your soup without having to search the spice rack. They are usually salty, so one package goes a long way

Rice and pasta. These can bulk up soups, but if they're left sitting in hot broth for very long, they absorb too much liquid and turn mushy. That's fine if you want thickness and texture. But otherwise, allow just enough time for the rice or pasta to cook before serving time.

Bagged, peeled carrots. When the peeling is already done for you, it seems a simple matter to slice them. But you can also buy carrots presliced. I like to buy matchstick-cut carrots—thin little shards that are easy to sauté or simmer. In the case of several of my stew recipes, you can throw in whole baby carrots.

Spices and herbs. Most of my soups contain commonly used herbs and spices, because their fragrant aromas and subtle flavors add complexity to your soups. A sprinkle of chopped herbs such as parsley, cilantro, or basil at the end of cooking time adds color as well. And researchers are finding evidence that spices and herbs help boost the antioxidant power of your food— just one more reason to spice it up.

If you're not sure how a spice or herb will taste, ladle a half cup of the soup mixture into a bowl and stir in a half teaspoon of the seasoning. Wait a minute and taste test it. It may save you from ruining a whole batch of soup.

Err on the side of too little seasoning or salt, then taste just before serv-ing and add more if necessary. If you go overboard with too much seasoning, you can end up with food that's bitter, pungent, or too hot. It's easier to add more to the soup than subtract it, which is often impossible.

Seasoning blends, such as Italian herbs, Greek seasoning, curry powder, and spice rubs make it easy to add flavor. Look for a mix that doesn't contain salt; you can always add it if you need it.

If you are wary of investing in jars of expensive spices that will sit unused in the cupboard, buy the smallest sized jars that hold less than an ounce. Although they cost more per ounce, you're more likely to use them up before their flavor diminishes.

Fresh herbs can be expensive. I like to grow some of my favorites (basil, rosemary, and thyme) year-round in my windowsill so I can quickly snip off a few sprigs at a time.

I've tried to stick to fairly common herbs and spices for most of these recipes. They include:

Black pepper. The most commonly used spice worldwide, its extracts were used as a folk medicine in many cultures. A hint of pepper perks up just about anything, from vegetables to pasta to salad.

Curry powder. This spice mix typically includes golden turmeric, coriander, cumin, fenugreek, and red pepper. Unless you use enough curry to warrant mixing these ingredients on your own, buy a jar of already mixed powder.

Oregano. A Mediterranean mainstay, it has one of the highest antioxidant levels of all dried herbs. It's also used in Mexican dishes.

Cumin. This earthy spice is found in many cuisines, from Mexican to North African to Indian. It's a critical ingredient of chili powder and is found in curry powder, garam masala, and adobo seasonings.

Red chile pepper. Some studies indicate that spicing up your meal with cayenne, chiles, and paprika can help boost your metabolism as well as give your soup a little kick. When people added red pepper to their food, they ate fewer calories during that meal—and even during the next meal. Just be careful to stay within your comfort level, heat-wise.

Ginger. This pungent, citrusy flavored spice has as many antioxidants as a cup of spinach.

Thyme. A teaspoon of this versatile herb is also high in antioxidants. A pinch of thyme is great, but too much makes a dish taste harsh and bitter.

Rosemary. This classic Italian herb imparts a piney flavor. In ancient Greece, rosemary was thought to strengthen the brain and memory, and modern-day research has linked it to protection against brain degeneration.

Basil. This Italian herb is rich in antioxidants and contains oils that prevent bacteria growth and inflammation. Basil stars in Italian soups and pesto.

Bay leaf. In ancient Greece, champions of the Olympic games wore garlands of bay leaves. One or two leaves per soup is all you need; remove the leaves before serving.

Nutmeg. While nutmeg is seen as a "sweet" spice used in pumpkin pie, it's also a stealth ingredient used to perk up soups and savory dishes too.

Paprika. In America, we tend to limit paprika to a sprinkle on potato salad or deviled eggs. But it's popular in other countries, such as Hungary, for its vibrant color and rich, earthy flavor.

SOUP GLOSSARY

So when does soup become stew or bisque or chowder? Here are some basic definitions, based on *The Food Lover's Companion*, by Sharon Tyler Herbst. But often the terms can be interchangeable.

Soup: Any combination of meat, vegetables, fruit, and/or fish cooked in a liquid.

Stew: A dish containing meat and vegetables with a thick broth made from the cooking liquid and natural juices of the food being cooked.

Bisque: A thick, rich soup usually consisting of pureed seafood and cream.

Chili: A spicy stew-like soup, usually flavored with chiles or chili powder.

Chowder: A thick, chunky soup, usually containing seafood.

Consommé: Thin, clear broth.

Gumbo: A thick stew that can include shellfish, meats, okra, tomatoes, and onion. A Creole specialty, it is a mainstay of New Orleans cuisine.

Hearty Chicken Noodle Soup 2

Slow Cooker Chicken and Chives Stew................................ 4

Turkey and Wild Rice Soup 5

Salsa Chicken Soup.. 6

Old-Fashioned Chicken Vegetable Soup 8

Thai-Style Chicken Soup 10

Chicken Gnocchi Soup 12

Cilantro Lime Rice and Chicken Soup 13

Chipotle White Chicken Chili................................ 14

Chicken Cacciatore (Hunter's Stew) 16

Cheddar Chicken and Broccoli Soup 18

Chicken Fajita Soup with Lime 20

Turkey Pot Pie Soup.. 22

Easy Homemade Turkey Broth 23

Post-Thanksgiving Turkey Chili 24

Chicken Potato Florentine 26

Slow Cooker Nacho Chicken Soup........................... 28

Avgolemono—Greek Egg Lemon Soup 30

Mulligatawny.. 32

Quick Creamy Chicken Noodle Soup....................... 33

Quick Chicken Tortilla Soup with Avocado 34

Chicken Paprikás.. 36

Slow Cooker Homemade Chicken Broth 38

POULTRY SOUPS

HEARTY CHICKEN NOODLE SOUP

This comfort-classic sports chunks of white meat, lots of noodles, and a flavorful broth. The prep time is slashed with canned broth and frozen carrots, celery, and onion. You can save another five or ten minutes by using the meat from an already cooked rotisserie chicken.

1 Tbsp. oil

3 raw chicken breasts, partially frozen (or 3 C. of cooked rotisserie chicken)

1 12-oz. pkg. frozen mirepoix blend (or 2/3 C. fresh chopped onion, 1/3 C. sliced celery, and 1/3 C. chopped carrots)

5 14-oz. cans (or about 7 C.) chicken stock

2 tsp. dried minced onion

1 Tbsp. garlic powder

1 tsp. dried thyme

1 bay leaf

5 to 8 oz. (about 1/3 to half of a 1-lb. pkg.) dry linguini, spaghetti, or egg noodles

1 Tbsp. tomato paste, optional

1 tsp. freshly ground pepper, more to taste

1 tsp. dried parsley, or 1 Tbsp. fresh parsley

1. Heat oil in a 4-to-6-quart stockpot over low heat while you dice the chicken. On a cutting board, cut the chicken breasts in 1-inch cubes with a sharp knife. This is easier to do when chicken is partially frozen. (If using rotisserie chicken, pull breast and thigh meat from the chicken and dice it to total about 3 C.)

2. Turn heat to high, place raw chicken in pot, and cook about 5 minutes, stirring occasionally, until lightly browned.

3. Add frozen vegetables. Cook for another 5 minutes, stirring occasionally.

4. Add chicken stock, onion, garlic powder, thyme, and bay leaf (and rotisserie chicken, if you're using it) and bring mixture to a gentle boil.

5. Break noodles into 2-inch lengths and add to soup with tomato paste (if desired), pepper, and parsley. Cook about 10 minutes or until noodles are tender.

Options: For a richer flavor, substitute thigh or leg meat for chicken breasts.

SLOW COOKER CHICKEN AND CHIVES STEW

Prep time: 15 minutes, Cooking time: 6 1/2–8 hours | *Makes about 6 1 1/2-cup servings*

Don't worry that there's not enough liquid in this stew. The heat will release the natural moisture in the vegetables, and it won't evaporate while the lid is on the slow cooker. An hour before serving, check the stew, and if it seems too thin, leave the lid off so the moisture can evaporate. If it seems too thick, add a little more water or chicken broth and leave the lid on.

Nonstick cooking spray

1 1/2 C. frozen green peppers, or 1 green or red bell pepper

2 large potatoes

2 lbs. boneless, skinless chicken thighs or breasts, partially frozen (I like to use a combination of both, about 4–5 thighs and 1 breast)

2 Tbsp. dehydrated onion flakes

1 1-lb. bag baby carrots

1 can cream of chicken soup

1 C. water

4 chicken bouillon cubes

1 Tbsp. Montreal chicken seasoning (Weber or McCormick), optional

1 tsp. freshly ground pepper

1 8-oz. tub of onion-and-chive-flavored cream cheese

1 tsp. dried minced chives, optional

Spray a slow cooker with nonstick cooking spray. On a cutting board with a sharp chef's knife, slice peppers into thin strips. Peel potatoes and dice into 1 1/2-inch chunks. Dice the chicken into 1 1/2-inch pieces. This is easier to do if chicken is partially frozen.

Place all ingredients in slow cooker, with cream cheese on top. Cover and cook 4–5 hours on high, 6–8 hours on low. After stew has been cooking a few hours, stir to mix all ingredients evenly. You may want to remove lid during last hour of cooking for thicker stew.

TURKEY AND WILD RICE SOUP

Prep time: 25 minutes | *Makes about 6 1 1/2-cup servings*

This is a great post-Thanksgiving soup, with the wild rice mix giving a quick flavor and texture boost. Don't throw out the leftover drippings from roasting your turkey; add it to the soup for a richer broth.

1. Melt butter in a 4-quart stockpot over low heat while slicing celery and carrots, and dicing the turkey breast into 1/2-inch pieces.

2. Turn heat to high and add vegetables to pot. Cook, stirring occasionally, about 5 minutes, until celery is translucent.

3. Add turkey, bacon, water, and broth to pot. Cover with lid and turn heat to high until mixture comes to a boil, about 3 minutes.

4. Stir in rice mix and seasoning packet. Turn heat to medium, cover with lid, and cook 5 minutes. Turn off heat and allow soup to stand another 5 minutes before serving.

1 Tbsp. butter or margarine
1 C. celery, sliced (about 2 stalks)
1 C. carrots, sliced (or use about 1 1/2 C. frozen sliced carrots)
1 lb. cooked turkey breast, diced (about 2–3 C.)
1 3-oz. pkg. or jar real bacon pieces (about 3/4 C.)
5 C. water
1 14-oz. can chicken or turkey broth (or about 1 C. of turkey stock left over from roasting the turkey, plus 3/4 C. water)
1 6.2-oz. box fast-cooking long-grain-and-wild-rice mix with seasoning packet (such as Uncle Ben's Original)

SALSA CHICKEN SOUP

Prep time: 30 minutes (less if you use already cooked chicken) | *Makes about 6 1 1/2-cup servings*

My family's favorite soup is also a perfect cold-buster: the traditional chicken soup cure-all with a boost of head-clearing chiles. Most of the ingredients come straight from your pantry. The minute or two spent snipping fresh cilantro is worth it; dried cilantro flakes are flavorless.

2 boneless, skinless chicken breasts (about 2 to 3 C. cooked, diced chicken)
1 Tbsp. vegetable oil
1 Tbsp. dried chopped onion
2 tsp. garlic powder
1 Tbsp. ground cumin (or half a packet of Mexican seasoning if you omit the onion and garlic powder)
2 14-oz. cans of chicken broth (or 4 C. water with 4 chicken bouillon cubes)
1 24-oz. jar mild or medium chunky salsa (hotter if desired)
1 7-oz. can diced mild green chiles (or jalapeños if you desire more heat)
1 15-oz. can corn, drained
2 15-oz. cans black beans, rinsed and drained
1/2 C. chopped fresh cilantro
1 bag baked tortilla chips
Shredded cheddar cheese or light sour cream for garnish, if desired

1. Dice chicken breasts into 1-inch cubes (this is easier to do when chicken is partially frozen).

2. Brown chicken in oil in a 4-to-6-quart stockpot over medium-high heat, adding onion as chicken begins to brown.

3. Add garlic, cumin, water, broth, salsa, chiles, corn, black beans, and half of cilantro. Bring mixture to a gentle boil and cook 10–15 minutes or until chicken is cooked through.

4. To serve, put a few chips in each bowl then ladle soup into bowl. Sprinkle with remaining cilantro and/or cheddar cheese, and add sour cream and tortilla strips, if desired.

Slow Cooker Option: Put all ingredients in cooker except for half of cilantro. Cook on high 3–4 hours, or on low 5–7 hours. Add remaining cilantro at the end of cooking time.

Options: If you have leftover soup, make a Salsa Chicken Rice Casserole by stirring in cooked rice, topping with cheddar or Monterey Jack cheese. This soup freezes well.

OLD-FASHIONED CHICKEN VEGETABLE SOUP

Prep time: 35 minutes (less if using cooked chicken and frozen vegetables) | *Makes 8 to 9 1 1/2-cup servings*

Salad haters can get in their quota of veggies with this satisfying soup. The recipe takes thirty-five minutes if you're cutting up fresh chicken and vegetables; you'll save time by using leftover or rotisserie-cooked chicken and/or frozen vegetables. It's much easier to dice raw chicken if it's partially frozen.

1 Tbsp. vegetable oil
2 large, partially frozen, boneless, skinless chicken breasts, or 1 breast and 2 boneless, skinless thighs, diced into 1-inch pieces (or 2 to 3 C. cooked, diced chicken)
3 14-oz. cans chicken broth (or 5 C. water with 5 chicken bouillon cubes)
1 C. thinly sliced celery, about 2 ribs
2 C. baby carrots, cut into chunks (or about 2 1/2 C. frozen sliced carrots)
2 large potatoes, peeled and diced in 1-inch cubes (or 1 20-oz. pkg. of Simply Potatoes fresh-cut potatoes, or 4 C. frozen diced hash browns)
1/4 C. dried chopped onion
1 tsp. garlic powder
1 tsp. dried thyme
1 bay leaf
1 14.5-oz. can diced tomatoes
1 tsp. freshly ground pepper
1 C. corn kernels, canned or frozen
1 C. frozen peas
Salt to taste

1. Heat oil in large stockpot over low heat while you dice chicken into 1-inch pieces.

2. Turn heat to high and cook chicken until no longer pink and begins to turn golden brown.

3. Add broth (or water and bouillon cubes) and bring soup to a gentle boil.

4. While soup comes to a boil, slice celery and carrots and add to pot.

5. Peel and dice potatoes (if using fresh). Add fresh or frozen potatoes to pot along with onion flakes, garlic, thyme, bay leaf, tomatoes, pepper, and corn.

6. Keep soup at a gentle boil for 15 more minutes, or until meat and vegetables are tender.

7. Taste and correct seasonings; you may want to add salt, more garlic, broth, thyme, or pepper, depending on individual taste. Add peas as you take the soup off the heat, so they don't lose their bright color.

Options: Add 1 C. dried pasta such as broken spaghetti, rotini, or penne about 10 minutes before serving. You can also add other vegetables such as chopped red or green pepper, frozen green beans, or chopped parsley.

Slow cooker option: Place all ingredients except peas in slow cooker. Cook on high 3–4 hours or low 6–8 hours. Add peas just before serving.

THAI-STYLE CHICKEN SOUP

Prep time: 30 minutes | Makes about 6 1 1/2-cup servings

This soup is a nod to Tom Ka Gai soup served in Asian restaurants, without the prep work of fresh lemongrass, kaffir lime leaves, chiles, and galangal. You can find tubes of crushed lemon grass, such as the Gourmet Garden brand, in most grocery store produce departments. A little jar of red curry paste (such as the Thai Kitchen brand found in the Asian foods aisle of your grocery store) contains the Kaffir lime leaves, galangal, and red chiles. If you don't like much heat, the green curry paste is an option. Fresh cilantro is a must; dried cilantro has no flavor.

1 Tbsp. vegetable oil
1 C. frozen chopped onion
1 C. sliced button mushrooms
2 14-oz. cans chicken broth
1/4 C. crushed lemongrass
2 tsp. Thai red curry paste (or use green curry if you want more heat)
2 1/2 C. chopped, cooked chicken breast (can be from a rotisserie chicken or frozen oven-roasted chicken, about 2 chicken breasts)
2 14-oz. cans unsweetened coconut milk (can use light coconut milk)
1 tsp. dried, powdered ginger
2 Tbsp. lime juice (frozen, bottled, or fresh-squeezed from 1 lime)
1/2 of a red bell pepper, julienned (about 1/2 C.)

1/2 C. chopped cilantro leaves, and more for garnish
2 Tbsp. sugar
Salt to taste

1. Heat vegetable oil in a skillet over medium-high heat. Add onion and cook, stirring occasionally.

2. While onion is cooking, place sliced mushrooms on a cutting board and coarsely chop. Add mushrooms; stir and cook for about 5 minutes.

3. Add chicken broth, lemongrass, curry paste, chicken, coconut milk, ginger, and lime juice. Simmer about 20 minutes.

4. While soup is simmering, slice the red bell pepper into thin strips, about 1/2 inch wide and 1 to 2 inches long. Add to the soup.

5. Chop the cilantro leaves and add to soup, along with sugar.

Taste and add salt as needed. Add more curry paste or lemon grass if desired.

Options: Add 2 tsp. fish sauce (nam pla) for a strong, salty flavor. You can also add vegetables such as 1 C. snow peas, 1 C. green beans, 1 C. chopped broccoli, or 1 C. finely chopped carrots to the soup during the simmering period.

CHICKEN GNOCCHI SOUP

Prep time: 20 minutes | Makes about 6 1 1/4-cup servings

Gnocchi (pronounced NYAW kee) are little Italian dumplings made with potato and wheat flour. You can find them in the pasta section at your grocery store. They don't need much time to cook—just four to five minutes—so this soup comes together quickly. Using rotisserie chicken, leftover cooked chicken, or frozen roasted chicken breast makes it even faster. The fresh spinach adds color as well as nutrition.

2 pkg. Alfredo sauce mix
3 C. milk
1 14-oz. can chicken broth
1/4 C. butter
1–2 tsp. parsley flakes
2 tsp. garlic powder
2 to 3 C. cooked chicken breast, cubed
   or shredded
1 16-oz. pkg. gnocchi
1 C. chopped spinach, packed
Salt and pepper to taste

1. Stir together Alfredo sauce mix, milk, chicken broth, butter, parsley flakes, and garlic powder in a 4-to-6-quart stockpot over medium-high heat.

2. When mixture comes to a gentle boil, add chicken and gnocchi. Allow mixture to boil gently for about 4 minutes, or until gnocchi is tender.

3. Turn down the heat to medium so mixture simmers.

4. Chop fresh spinach on a cutting board and stir into soup. Add salt and pepper to taste.

5. If the consistency is too thick for your taste, thin it with milk or broth before serving.

CILANTRO LIME RICE AND CHICKEN SOUP

Prep time: 20 minutes | Makes about 6 1 1/2-cup servings

Fresh cilantro adds Southwestern flair to this spicy soup. Don't waste your money on dried cilantro, as it has very little flavor. This soup comes together fast with rotisserie chicken. You can also use leftover cooked chicken, or frozen roasted chicken pieces (such as Tyson). Beans, rice, and corn make this a hearty one-pot meal.

1. Place broth in a 4-to-6-quart stockpot over high heat. Add rice and bring to a gentle boil.

2. Meanwhile, remove chicken from carcass of rotisserie chicken (or use frozen grilled chicken). Cut it into 1-inch pieces and add to the pot.

3. As rice cooks, add onion, garlic powder, cumin, tomatoes, corn, black beans, 2 Tbsp. cilantro, lime juice, and sugar.

4. Cook for about 15 minutes, until rice is tender. If soup becomes too thick, thin with a little water.

5. Serve with a sprinkle of remaining 2 Tbsp. cilantro, cheddar cheese, sour cream, olives, and so on.

2 14-oz. cans of chicken broth (or 4 C. water with 4 chicken bouillon cubes)

1/2 C. long-grain white rice

2 C. cooked, diced chicken (from a rotisserie chicken, leftovers, or frozen roasted chicken pieces such as Tyson)

2 Tbsp. dried chopped onion

2 tsp. garlic powder

1 Tbsp. ground cumin (or use a half packet of Mexican seasoning and omit onion and garlic powder)

2 10-oz. cans diced tomatoes with chiles (Ro-Tel)

1 15-oz. can corn, drained

1 15-oz. can black beans, rinsed and drained

1/4 C. chopped fresh cilantro, divided

1 Tbsp. lime juice

1 Tbsp. brown sugar

CHIPOTLE WHITE CHICKEN CHILI

Prep time: 30 minutes | Makes about 6 1-1/2-cup servings

Chipotle chiles—smoked jalapeño peppers—are found in the Mexican food aisle, in seven-ounce cans with adobo sauce. You only need one or two chiles for this dish, but don't let the rest of the can go to waste; freeze it and then shave off a bit every time you need to add a little smoky kick to a dish. If you prefer, you can make this chili with rotisserie chicken or frozen, cooked, and diced chicken pieces. Pull the meat off a rotisserie chicken and dice it into one-inch pieces or shred it apart with your fingers. Either way, you should have two and a half to thee cups of chicken meat.

1 Tbsp. canola oil
2 large boneless, skinless chicken
   breasts
3 14-oz. cans chicken broth
2 Tbsp. dried chopped onion
1 tsp. garlic powder
2 tsp. ground cumin
1 tsp. oregano
1/2 tsp. ground cayenne pepper or
   chili powder (more if desired)
2 7-oz. cans diced green chiles
1 or 2 chipotle chiles, canned in adobo
   sauce, and 1 Tbsp. adobo sauce
2 15-oz. cans Great Northern beans
   or other white beans, drained and
   well rinsed
1/2 C. chopped cilantro
Salt and pepper to taste
Shredded cheese
Tortilla chips

1. Heat oil in a 4-quart stockpot on high.

2. Add chicken breasts and sauté until golden brown on both sides, about 5–8 minutes.

3. Remove chicken to a cutting board to cool.

4. Add chicken broth, onion, garlic powder, cumin, oregano, cayenne or chili powder, green and chipotle chiles, adobo sauce, and beans to pot. With potato masher, mash some of the beans to create a thicker soup. Allow soup to simmer 10 minutes.

5. While soup is simmering, dice cooked chicken breasts into 1-inch cubes.

6. Add chicken to pot and cook an additional 5 minutes while you chop cilantro.

7. Add cilantro just before serving. Taste and add more salt, pepper, or chili powder if desired. Serve topped with shredded cheese or tortilla chips.

Options: If you have more time, roast and dice fresh chiles instead of using canned.

CHICKEN CACCIATORE (HUNTER'S STEW)

Prep time: 35 minutes | Makes 6 servings; about 1 cup stew plus 1/2 cup rice each

This Italian favorite usually takes several hours for the chicken to braise, the sauce to slowly thicken, and flavors to blend. I cut to the chase by using boneless, skinless chicken thighs, which cook quickly and are flavorful and tender. Tomato paste gives thickness and adds to the "braised" flavor. For those who don't like the textures of olives, mushrooms, zucchini, or artichokes, you can puree them in the blender with some of the canned tomatoes then add to the stew. You'll have the flavor without the texture.

1 Tbsp. oil
2 lbs. boneless, skinless chicken thighs
1 1/2 C. frozen green pepper (or 1 large chopped green or red bell pepper)
1 C. frozen onion
1 Tbsp. garlic powder
1 14.5-oz. can petite-diced tomatoes
2 tsp. sugar
1 can tomato paste
1 14-oz. can chicken broth
1 Tbsp. Italian seasoning (or 1 tsp. basil, 1 tsp. oregano, and 1 tsp. rosemary)
1 1/2 C. medium- or long-grain rice
3 1/4 C. water
1/2 C. Kalamata olives
1 medium zucchini
1 can mushrooms (or about 1 C. fresh sliced mushrooms)
1 C. canned artichoke hearts, drained, optional

1. Heat oil over low heat while cutting each thigh in half horizontally then lengthwise, making 4 pieces per thigh.

2. Turn heat to medium-high and add chicken. Cook, stirring occasionally, about 5 minutes.

3. While chicken is cooking, chop bell peppers if using fresh. Turn heat to high and add pepper and onion to chicken.

4. Cook chicken, onion, and pepper about 5 more minutes, or until chicken is browned.

5. Add garlic powder, tomatoes, sugar, paste, chicken broth, and Italian seasoning. Cook, stirring occasionally, for 10 minutes.

6. While stew cooks, mix rice and water together in a microwavable casserole dish with lid. Cook on high, covered, for 5 minutes, or until water is boiling. Turn setting to medium-low, remove the lid, and microwave for 12–15 more minutes, or until rice is tender.

7. While rice and stew are cooking, chop or slice the olives. Cut each olive in half lengthwise and add to stew. Place zucchini on a cutting board and cut it in half lengthwise, then slice each half into 1/4-inch-thick slices. Add to pot. Add mushrooms. Drain canned artichokes and pour onto a cutting board. Chop into 1/2-inch pieces and add to pot. Cook 5–10 more minutes.

8. Serve 1 C. of stew over 1/2 C. of cooked rice, per serving.

CHEDDAR CHICKEN AND BROCCOLI SOUP

Prep time: 30 minutes | *Makes about 6 1 1/2-cup servings*

Chicken, cheese, and broccoli are a triple combination for a hot, hearty soup. Frozen onions and hash browns make it quick fix. Extra-sharp cheddar adds lots of flavor.

1 Tbsp. canola oil
1 large boneless, skinless chicken breast or 3 boneless, skinless thighs (about 2 C. uncooked, diced chicken)
1/4 C. dried minced onion
4 C. frozen Southern-style hash browns
2 14-oz. cans chicken broth
2 C. milk
1 12-oz. pkg. frozen chopped broccoli
1 tsp. garlic powder
1 tsp. freshly ground pepper
2 Tbsp. cornstarch
1/4 C. water
2 1/2 C. shredded extra-sharp cheddar, divided
Salt to taste

1. Warm oil in a 4- to 6-quart stockpot over low heat while you dice chicken into 1-inch pieces. This is easier to do if chicken is partially frozen.

2. When chicken is diced, turn heat to high and add chicken. Let chicken sear so outside is golden brown.

3. Turn heat to medium-high and add onion, potatoes, broth, and milk. Allow soup to come to a gentle boil. Cook about 5 minutes.

4. Stir in chopped broccoli, garlic powder, and pepper. Turn heat to high to allow soup to come back to a gentle boil. Cook an additional 10 minutes, until broccoli and potatoes are tender.

5. In a small cup, mix cornstarch and water into a smooth paste. Stir into boiling soup. Keep stirring as mixture thickens.

6. Turn off heat and add 2 C. cheddar cheese, stirring until cheese is melted and well blended.

7. Taste; add salt and more pepper if desired.

Top each serving with a spoonful of remaining cheese.

CHICKEN FAJITA SOUP WITH LIME

Prep time: 30 minutes | Makes 6 1 1/2-cup servings

Using already diced, cooked chicken makes this Southwestern-flavored soup easy to make. Roasting the fresh chiles can be done quickly right in the stockpot before the soup is made, to avoid washing another pan. You can also substitute shrimp or beef for the chicken if you want. You will want to use fresh onion and pepper because they will caramelize while cooking to help flavor the soup.

3 New Mexico or Anaheim long green chiles
1 Tbsp. canola oil
2 yellow onions
1 red bell pepper
1 green bell pepper
3 14-oz. cans chicken broth
2 to 3 C. sliced or diced cooked chicken (frozen or rotisserie)
2 tsp. powdered garlic
1 Tbsp. cumin (or taco seasoning)
1 lime (for both zest and juice)
1 tsp. sugar
Garnish: chopped tomatoes, salsa, sour cream etc.

1. Heat a 4- to-6-quart stockpot over high. Cut the tops off chiles and lay on bottom of stockpot. Push down slightly with spatula to flatten chiles. When bottom sides of chiles have brown spots and blisters (about 2–3 minutes), use tongs to turn each chile over so other side can roast, for about 2 more minutes. Try to rotate each chile so most of skin gets blistered. Turn off heat. With tongs, place chiles in container with tight-fitting lid. Let sit for about 10 minutes to engage peel.

2. While chiles are sitting, pour 1 Tbsp. oil in bottom of empty stockpot to warm over low heat while you slice onions and bell peppers into thin strips.

3. Turn the heat to high and sauté onions and bell peppers for 5–10 minutes, until limp and slightly browned on edges.

4. Add broth, chicken, garlic powder, and cumin. While broth comes to a boil, use a zester or the fine-holed side of a grater to zest outer green skin of the lime. Add zest to soup. Cut lime in half; squeeze juice and add to soup with sugar.

5. Let soup simmer while you remove chiles from container. Place on a cutting board, cut top off each chile and make a vertical slit down side to open each chile. Scrape off seeds with flat edge of a knife. Lift off the peel along the blisters of the chiles. Dice each chile and add to soup. (Wash your hands after handling chiles to avoid burns). Cook an additional 5 minutes to blend the flavors. Serve with tortilla strips, cheese, sour cream, salsa, olives, or lime wedges.

TURKEY POT PIE SOUP

Prep time: 30 minutes | *Makes about 6 1 1/2-cup servings*

This is a wonderful day-after-Thanksgiving meal, using leftover turkey and leftover piecrust.
But it's also good anytime! You can use roasted, diced chicken or beef as well.

4 C. turkey or chicken broth

2 Tbsp. dried chopped onion

3 to 4 C. frozen hash browns O'Brien

3 to 4 C. diced, cooked turkey (can be white or dark meat, or both)

3-oz. pkg. real bacon pieces, optional

3 to 4 C. frozen mixed vegetables (corn, peas, carrots, and green beans)

1 4-oz. can mushroom stems and pieces, drained

2 Tbsp. cornstarch

1 8-oz. pkg. cream cheese

1 1/2 tsp. freshly ground pepper

Salt to taste

1 refrigerated piecrust

1. Heat broth in a 4-quart stockpot. Add onion, potatoes, turkey, bacon, vegetables, and mushrooms. Bring to a boil.

2. Mix cornstarch with 1/4 C. cold water until well blended. Whisk into soup and continue whisking as mixture boils and thickens, about 2–3 minutes.

3. Turn heat to medium-low. Cut cream cheese into smaller chunks and stir in into soup until well blended. Add pepper. Simmer an additional 10–15 minutes.

4. While soup simmers, unroll piecrust on baking sheet. With knife, cut crust into 6 or 7 3-by-3-inch squares (a good idea to make a spare in case one square breaks.) There will be some leftover dough scraps. Bake squares and leftover pieces at 425 degrees for 8–10 minutes, or until golden.

5. Serve each bowl of soup topped with a square of piecrust. The baked, leftover pieces can be used for dippers as well.

EASY HOMEMADE TURKEY BROTH

Prep time: 6–8 hours, Active time: 30 minutes | Makes about 4–5 cups broth

You can take advantage of a turkey carcass that you were going to toss out, save a little money, and control what's in your final product. The only difference is that it's hard to stuff the carcass from a 20-lb. turkey into a slow cooker. If you have a large turkey, you're better off using a big pot on the stovetop. When you prepare a vegetable/relish tray for Thanksgiving, think ahead and save the celery and carrot trimmings to use in your turkey broth-making.

1. Break or cut up turkey carcass and place in a large stockpot with remaining ingredients. Allow water to simmer for 3–4 hours, partially covered.

2. Allow the broth to cool for about an hour, then pour the liquid through a strainer and discard bones.

3. Simmer an additional 2–3 hours, uncovered, so that broth condenses.

4. Allow it to cool, then refrigerate for an hour, so fat hardens on top.

5. Skim hardened fat. Heat and serve as is, use it when making soup, or freeze for later use.

1 turkey carcass, with clinging bits of meat and skin, and pan drippings
10–12 C. cold water, enough to cover carcass
1 C. sliced celery (including leafy tops if you have them)
1 C. carrot chunks
1/4 C. dried minced onion (or 1 sliced fresh onion)
2 bay leaves
2 tsp. garlic powder
1 tsp. freshly ground pepper
1 tsp. salt
1 tsp. dried rosemary

POST-THANKSGIVING TURKEY CHILI

Prep time: 30 minutes (less if using canned chiles) | *Makes 6 1 1/2-cup servings*

This is a great holiday tradition, but don't limit yourself to Thanksgiving. You might even want to roast a couple of turkeys when they are at bargain prices during the holidays and freeze the meat for later use. Then use the carcass to make Turkey Broth, another recipe in this book. The recipe has a quick way to "roast" chiles. But you can skip that process and use 2 four-ounce cans of mild green chiles if you want.

3 Anaheim chiles
1 Tbsp. butter
2 C. frozen onion, partially thawed
2 cans Ro-Tel tomatoes and chiles, original
4 C. diced turkey
3 15-oz. cans black beans, drained and rinsed, or 4 C. cooked beans
3 1/2 C. homemade turkey stock (or 2 14-oz. cans of turkey or chicken broth)
1 Tbsp. cumin
2 tsp. paprika
1/2 tsp. chipotle powder, optional
1/4 C. fresh cilantro
1/2 tsp. sugar
1 envelope turkey gravy mix (optional)
1/2 C. sour cream

1. Place a nonstick 4-6-quart stockpot on high heat. Cut tops off chiles and lay them across bottom of the pan. As skins darken and blister, use tongs to press on chiles to flatten them to roast more evenly. Cook each side about 2 minutes, or until they have large blisters on them. Remove from heat and place in sealed plastic container.

2. Add the butter and onion to the hot pot and stir, about 2–3 minutes. Add tomatoes, turkey, beans, stock, and seasonings. Bring to a boil. Lower heat to medium and cook, covered, for 10 minutes.

3. While chili is cooking, remove roasted chiles from container to cutting board. Pull on blistered skin and lift off. With a knife, slit each chile vertically from top to bottom to open it up. Use the knife to scrape out seeds. Place chiles on top of each other and slice them, first horizontally then vertically to make small dices. You should have about 1 C. of diced and partially peeled chiles. Add to pot. (Wash your hands after handling chiles.)

4. Cook chili about 5–10 minutes more. Remove from heat. Ladle each serving and top with heaping spoonful of sour cream to swirl into soup.

CHICKEN POTATO FLORENTINE

Prep time: 30 minutes | *Makes about 6 1 1/2-cup servings*

The sun-dried tomatoes in this soup impart a sweeter, deeper flavor than fresh or canned tomatoes. Sun-dried tomatoes are usually found in the supermarket produce section. Don't use the oil-packed type. If you have a garden, it's a great idea to dry part of your tomato crop in the oven for future use in this soup, as well as in pasta or for snacking.

1 Tbsp. canola oil

2 C. frozen onion

4 C. frozen hash brown potatoes (or 2 medium-size russet potatoes, peeled and diced)

2 14-oz. cans chicken broth

2 C. milk or half-and-half (can be fat-free)

1 C. sun-dried tomatoes

2–3 C. chopped or diced cooked chicken or turkey (from leftovers, rotisserie chicken, or frozen precooked)

1 1.3-oz. envelope dry Alfredo sauce mix

1 Tbsp. Italian seasoning (or 1 tsp. basil, 1 tsp. oregano, 1 tsp. rosemary)

1 tsp. garlic powder

2 C. spinach, packed (more for garnish if desired)

Salt and freshly ground pepper to taste

1. Heat oil in a 4-to-6-quart stockpot. Add onion and sauté until limp, 4–5 minutes.

2. Add potatoes and chicken broth to pot and bring to gentle boil. Cook for about 10 minutes.

3. While potatoes are cooking, place milk or half-and-half in blender with sun-dried tomatoes. Wait a few minutes for tomatoes to soften. Then blend on low speed until tomatoes are chopped.

4. Add the tomato mixture, diced chicken, Alfredo sauce mix, and herbs to pot. Stir until well mixed. Bring soup to a gentle boil, stirring occasionally, until soup thickens and potatoes are tender.

5. While soup is cooking, pile spinach on a cutting board. Using a chef's knife, make several slices to cut spinach into thick ribbons.

6. When potatoes are tender, stir spinach into soup. Serve topped with extra ribbons of spinach if desired.

SLOW COOKER NACHO CHICKEN SOUP

Prep time: 10 minutes, Cook time: 4–5 hours | Makes 6 1 1/2-cup servings

When I became engaged to my husband, Kim, his brother's family invited us over to dinner. My new sister-in-law, Deanne Phillips, served Nacho Chicken Casserole, which was kind of trendy in the eighties. I liked it so much I've made it many times in the past twenty-eight years. This super easy soup incorporates the same ingredients, letting the crushed chips thicken the broth. To lower the calorie count, I've used reduced-fat versions of cream of chicken soup, sour cream, and baked chips with good results. Don't use fat-free sour cream; it won't melt into the soup and has a weird flavor. If you're watching your salt content, look for low-sodium versions of taco seasoning and cream of chicken soup.

About 1 1/2 lbs. boneless chicken
    breasts or thighs
2 14-oz. cans chicken broth
2 7-oz. cans diced green chiles
1 envelope taco seasoning
1 can condensed cream of chicken
    soup
1 C. sour cream
1/2 C. chopped fresh cilantro, divided
About 2 C. crushed nacho-flavored
    chips or baked tortilla chips
1 C. grated sharp cheddar cheese
Optional: 1 can black beans, drained
    and rinsed, and/or 1 can corn,
    drained
Garnishes: sliced olives, chopped red
    peppers

1. Place chicken, broth, chiles, taco seasoning, and cream of chicken soup in slow cooker, with lid.

2. Cook on high 3–4 hours, or on low 6–8 hours.

3. With a large slotted spoon, remove the chicken from the pot and place in a medium-sized bowl to cool slightly.

4. Stir the sour cream, 1/4 C. of the cilantro, chips, and cheese into the soup. You may also add the optional beans and corn.

5. With two large forks, shred chicken. Return chicken to pot and stir well before serving.

6. Serve each bowl with a sprinkling of cilantro, sliced olives, or chopped red peppers.

AVGOLEMONO—GREEK EGG LEMON SOUP

Prep time: 30 minutes | Makes about 6 1 1/2-cup servings

I was given this recipe by a Greek friend who yearns for her grandmother's (Yia Yia's) cooking but doesn't have the time to spend all day making it. In Greek, avgo *is "egg" and* lemono *is "lemon." By using rotisserie chicken, canned broth, and frozen lemon juice, it's streamlined while staying true to the traditional egg-thickened rice soup. She likes using converted rice (such as Uncle Ben's) because it doesn't go mushy during cooking. The lemon gives a bright, fragrant flavor to the broth. Don't skip the tempering step; it's essential to thickening the broth.*

3 14-oz. cans chicken broth
1 C. frozen onion
1 C. converted rice (such as Uncle Ben's)
1 rotisserie chicken
3 egg yolks
2 Tbsp. water
4 to 5 Tbsp. frozen or bottled lemon juice (or 2 freshly squeezed lemons)

1. Add onion, broth, and rice to a 4-to-6-quart stockpot and bring to a boil.

2. Remove rotisserie chicken meat from the carcass and dice so that you have about 2–3 cups of meat. Add to pot. Cook until rice is almost tender, about 10–15 minutes. Turn heat to a simmer.

3. With a whisk, beat egg yolks and water in a bowl. Add lemon juice, beating constantly.

4. Whisk in 1/4 C. of hot broth to egg-lemon mixture and stir well. (This is called tempering). Repeat process again with another ladleful of soup; then repeat again with one more ladle of soup.

5. Finally, stir egg mixture into the soup, whisking to blend well. Continue to let soup simmer for a few more minutes until it thickens. Do not boil. Add more salt and pepper, if desired, before serving.

MULLIGATAWNY

Prep time: 30 minutes | *Makes 6 1 1/2-cup servings*

This curry-flavored soup has roots in both East Indian and British cuisine. I sped up the process with frozen vegetables and frozen cooked, diced chicken. If the chicken is completely frozen, use three cups; if it's thawed, use two and a half cups. The lentils must be added early in the recipe: they need about twenty minutes to cook.

1 Tbsp. canola oil
1 12-oz. pkg. frozen mirepoix blend
    (or 2/3 C. fresh chopped onion,
    1/3 C. sliced celery, and 1/3 C.
    chopped carrots)
3 14-oz. cans chicken broth
1/2 C. lentils
2 C. frozen hash browns O'Brien
1 14-oz. can unsweetened coconut
    milk (light can be used)
1/2 C. shredded, sweetened coconut
1 Tbsp. curry powder
1/4 tsp. nutmeg
1 Tbsp. tomato paste
1 tsp. garlic powder
2 C. diced, cooked chicken (such as
    Tyson Oven-Roasted)

1. Heat oil in a 4-quart stockpot over medium-high heat. Add carrots, onion, and celery. Stir and cook 2–3 minutes.

2. Add chicken broth and lentils. Bring mixture to a gentle boil and cook about 5 minutes.

3. Add remaining ingredients and cook an additional 15 minutes or until lentils are tender.

Options: Add 1 peeled, cored, and chopped apple, or 1/2 C. chopped cashews or pistachios.

QUICK CREAMY CHICKEN NOODLE SOUP

Prep time: 20 minutes | *Makes about 6 1 1/2-cup servings*

In just twenty minutes you can be curled up with a cup of this comfort food. If you use light cream cheese, it will take a little longer to blend into the soup. Don't use fat-free cream cheese. It won't melt into the soup for the creamy consistency you want. If you want to add more vegetables, such as sliced carrots or celery, add them when you add the pasta so they will have enough time to cook.

1. Heat chicken broth in a 4-to-6-quart stockpot over high heat. Add chicken and onion flakes. Bring to a boil.

2. Holding both ends of pasta, break in thirds. When soup comes to a gentle boil, add pasta to soup. Cook 5 minutes.

3. Add cream cheese in chunks, and stir to melt and incorporate it into broth. It will take longer if you are using low-fat cream cheese.

4. In a cup, stir cornstarch and water together until there are no lumps. Whisk mixture into soup, and continue stirring as broth thickens.

5. Add parsley flakes and peas a few minutes before serving.

3 14-oz. cans chicken broth
4 C. frozen roasted cubed chicken breast (such as Tyson Oven-Roasted) or 3 C. cooked rotisserie chicken, shredded
2 Tbsp. dried minced onion flakes
4–6 oz. spaghetti or linguini pasta (about 1/4 of a 1-lb. pkg.)
1 cube cream cheese (can use light, or Neufchatel cream cheese)
3 Tbsp. cornstarch
1/2 C. water
2–3 tsp. dried parsley flakes
1/2 C. frozen peas

QUICK CHICKEN TORTILLA SOUP WITH AVOCADO

Prep time: 30 minutes | Makes about 6 1 1/2-cup servings

Just about every Mexican or Southwestern restaurant has a signature tortilla soup, all of them slightly different. This one has a clear broth and is studded with lots of smooth avocado chunks. The only time-consuming part is dicing the avocado. You could replace the avocado with a scoop of guacamole in each bowl, as some quick-serve Mexican restaurants do.

3 14-oz. cans chicken broth
2 cans tomatoes with chiles (Ro-Tel, original mild or hot, according to taste)
1 Tbsp. dried minced onion flakes
1 tsp. garlic powder
1 tsp. ground cumin
2-3 C. shredded rotisserie chicken meat
2 medium avocadoes, pitted, peeled, and chopped (or 1 1/2 C. guacamole)
1 1/2 C. crushed tortilla chips
1 C. shredded Monterey Jack cheese
1/4 C. chopped fresh cilantro
Lime wedges, optional

1. In 4-to-6-quart saucepan, heat broth, tomatoes, onion flakes, garlic powder, and cumin to boiling over medium-high heat.

2. While broth is heating, pull meat from rotisserie chicken, using your fingers or two forks to shred. Measure out 2 to 3 C. Add to pot and turn heat to medium and simmer broth for about 10 minutes.

3. While broth and chicken are simmering, peel and pit 2 avocados. Chop into 1/2-inch pieces.

4. Place cilantro in a measuring cup and snip with kitchen scissors until chopped.

5. Crush chips and divide among 6 serving bowls.

6. Spoon hot soup over chips, then top with avocado, cheese, and cilantro. Garnish each bowl with lime wedges, if desired.

CHICKEN PAPRIKÁS

Prep time: 40 minutes | *Makes 6 1-cup servings; about 1 cup stew per person, 1 1/2 cups if served over rice or pasta.*

The slow-simmered flavor of this Hungarian classic stew traditionally takes several hours, but with a few shortcuts it can be done in forty minutes, and half of that time is simply waiting. Boneless, skinless thighs cook quickly and remain tender and moist. In America, we tend to limit paprika to a sprinkle on potato salad or deviled eggs. But in Hungarian cooking, it lends vibrant color and a rich, earthy flavor, mellowed a bit by sour cream. We added carrots and peppers to make this dish a one-pot meal.

2 Tbsp. vegetable or olive oil
2 lbs. boneless, skinless chicken thighs (about 8 thighs), cut in quarters
2 C. frozen chopped onion
2 Tbsp. all-purpose flour
1 14-oz. can chicken broth
Half of a 1-lb. bag baby carrots
3 Tbsp. paprika (don't use hot or smoked paprika)
2 tsp. Mrs. Dash no-salt, all-purpose seasoning
1 14.5-oz. can petite-diced tomatoes
2 red bell peppers, stemmed, seeded, and diced
1 C. sour cream
2 Tbsp. fresh parsley or 2 tsp. parsley flakes
3 C. cooked pasta or rice for serving, optional

1. Heat oil over low heat in a 4-to-6-quart stockpot while you cut thighs in half.

2. Turn heat to high and add thighs to hot oil. Sauté until thighs are browned, about 5 minutes.

3. Add onion and continue to cook, stirring, until onion is limp, about 3 minutes.

4. Sprinkle the flour over the chicken and onion and stir until flour is well mixed.

5. Add the chicken broth, carrots, paprika, seasoning, and tomatoes. Stir well. Turn heat to medium-high and cover pot with a lid so mixture comes to gentle boil.

6. While the mixture cooks, slice bottom and top from the bell peppers so they are open cylinders. Cut slit down peppers to open them into a flat rectangle, and clean out seeds and white membrane. Place flat on cutting board and slice into strips. Chop up reserved bottom and top flesh of peppers as well. Add them to pot.

6. Keep soup at a gentle boil, stirring occasionally to prevent sticking, 15–20 minutes. While waiting, cook pasta or rice if desired. Mince parsley leaves on a cutting board, or by placing them in a measuring cup and snipping with kitchen shears.

7. When thighs and carrots are tender, stir in sour cream and parsley. Serve over pasta or rice if desired.

SLOW COOKER HOMEMADE CHICKEN BROTH

Prep time: 5–10 minutes, Cook time: 6–8 hours | Makes about 3–4 cups of chicken broth

Although commercially made chicken broth is convenient, it's not hard to make your own. Two ways to simplify: rotisserie chicken and your slow cooker. Every time you roast a chicken or buy a rotisserie-style chicken, you've got the perfect starting point for broth-making. On a cold, wintry day, simmering broth on the stove warms up your house with a steamy, delicious aroma. You can control what goes into it, if you want to avoid things like MSG, sodium, or wheat gluten. You can also save money and be environmentally conscious by using up bones and meat scraps that would otherwise be tossed. But it does take some simmering time. Often, homemade broth tastes weak and watery because it wasn't "reduced," or concentrated enough. By simmering it, uncovered, moisture evaporates. You end up with less volume but a more concentrated flavor. You can use the broth in other soups or on its own. A cup of steaming broth with a few crackers is a nice chill-chaser on a cold evening.

1 carcass from a roasted chicken, including clinging bits of meat
1 12-oz. pkg. frozen mirepoix blend (or 1/2 C. chopped onion, 1/3 C. chopped celery with leafy tops, and 1/3 C. chopped carrots— clean out your vegetable bin!)
1 tsp. garlic powder
1/2 tsp. salt
1/2 tsp. freshly ground pepper
1/2 tsp. dried thyme
1 bay leaf

1. Place carcass in the slow cooker and cover with cold water.

2. Add remaining ingredients. Place lid on slow cooker, turn on high, and leave for at least 4 hours.

3. Take off lid, stir contents well. Turn slow cooker to high and leave for 3–4 more hours so some of the liquid evaporates. Stir broth occasionally to keep a "skin" from forming on top, which will keep liquid from evaporating.

4. Turn off heat to allow broth to cool for an hour.

5. Place a strainer over a large bowl and pour out liquid, bones, and spent meat and vegetables. The strainer will catch the messy bones, leaving you with clean broth in the bowl.

6. Set bowl in refrigerator to chill overnight. The fat will float to top and harden, making it easy to skim with a spoon or spatula. Don't be alarmed that broth is gel-like when cold; it's supposed to be. It will liquefy once heated.

7. Taste broth and adjust seasonings. You may want to reduce it further by simmering. Use broth for soup that day or pour in airtight containers, label, and freeze for future use.

Slow-Cooked Beef Stew over Rice...................42

Beef Mushroom and Barley Stew......................43

Beefy Vegetable and Noodle Soup....................44

Beef and Biscuits 46

Terrific Taco Soup 48

RJ's Stuffed Pepper Soup...........................49

Rootin' Tootin' Cincinnati Chili...................50

Smoky Pork Chili Verde.............................52

Pasta and Ground Beef Soup 54

Italian Wedding Soup...............................55

Quick Tailgate Chili...............................56

Old-Fashioned Vegetable Beef Soup.................58

Beef Stroganoff Soup 60

Root Beer-Braised Beef Stew.......................61

Slow Cooker Smoky No-Bean Chili 62

Pepperoni Soupreme................................64

Savory Sausage Tortellini Soup 66

Presto Zuppa Toscana 67

Beef Borscht......................................68

Hungarian Goulash.................................70

BEEF AND PORK SOUPS

SLOW-COOKED BEEF STEW OVER RICE

Prep time: 10 minutes, Cooking time: 4–8 hours | Makes 6 servings, of about 1 cup rice and 1 cup beef stew per serving.

For an easy, no-fuss meal, simply toss most of the ingredients in a slow cooker. The vegetables break down into the broth, adding texture and flavor to the savory chunks of tender beef. A half hour before serving, cook the rice in the microwave, and thicken the beefy sauce with cornstarch.

2 lbs. beef stew meat
2 red or green bell peppers, diced
2 ribs of celery, sliced
1 1/2 C. frozen chopped onion (or about 1/4 C. dried chopped onion, or 1 C. chopped fresh onion)
3 beef bouillon cubes
1/4 C. soy sauce
2 1/2 C. water, divided
1 tsp. freshly ground pepper
2 Tbsp. cornstarch
For rice:
2 C. long-grain white rice
4 1/4 C. water
1/2 tsp. salt, optional

1. Place beef, bell pepper, celery, onion, bouillon, soy sauce, 2 C. of the water, and pepper in slow cooker.

2. Cover with lid. Cook for 4–5 hours on high or 6–8 hours on low.

3. About 30 minutes before serving, place rice and water in large, microwavable casserole bowl. Microwave on high, covered, for 5 minutes. Reduce power to medium-low (3 or 4 setting) and continue cooking, uncovered, for 15 more minutes or until tender.

4. About 25 minutes before serving, turn slow cooker to high. Mix cornstarch with 1/2 C. water. Whisk the cornstarch mixture into beef mixture until smooth. Allow mixture to cook, uncovered, about 15–20 more minutes to thicken. Serve beef stew over rice.

Option: You can serve the stew over baked potatoes instead of rice.

BEEF MUSHROOM AND BARLEY STEW

Prep time: 15 minutes | *Cooking time: 1 hour, 15 minutes*

This is a longer-cooking soup, but most of it is just waiting time. The stew meat, mushrooms, onion, and carrots are already sliced and diced. After that, you can forget about the soup until it's ready to serve.

1. Heat oil over high heat in a 4-to-6-quart nonstick pot, and sear meat so that it is browned on its surfaces, about 5 minutes.

2. Add rest of ingredients. Bring soup to a gentle boil. Reduce heat to medium and cover with a lid.

3. Cover and cook one hour or until meat is tender and barley is still a bit chewy.

Options: If you are able to find quick-cooking barley at your supermarket, you can make this soup in about half the time using leftover cooked beef and quick-cooking barley

1 Tbsp. canola oil
1 lb. precut beef stew meat, in 1–2-inch dices
8 oz. pkg. fresh sliced mushrooms
2 C. frozen diced onion
4 14-oz. cans beef broth
1 C. barley
2 C. fresh matchstick-cut carrots (or sliced carrots)
1 tsp. garlic powder
1 tsp. dried thyme
1/2 tsp. dried rosemary
2 bay leaves
1/4 C. tomato paste

BEEFY VEGETABLE AND NOODLE SOUP

Prep time: 30 minutes | Makes 6 1 1/2-cup servings

Instead of slow-simmering beef all day, just reach for a package of refrigerated beef tips with gravy. You can also make this soup with leftover roast beef and drippings. You'll want at least two cups of diced cooked beef and a half cup of drippings.

1 17-oz. pkg. refrigerated beef tips with gravy (such as Hormel)

1 16-oz. pkg. frozen mixed vegetables (such as carrots, corn, peas, and green beans)

2 C. frozen diced O'Brien-style hash browns

1 14.5-oz. can petite-diced tomatoes

1 Tbsp. dried chopped onion

6 beef bouillon cubes

1 bay leaf

6 C. water

Several grinds of fresh pepper

1 C. rotini pasta

1. Empty the package of beef tips into a 4-quart stockpot, using a spatula to get all the gravy.

2. Stir in vegetables, potatoes, tomatoes, onion, bouillon, bay leaf, water, and pepper. Bring to a boil.

3. Add pasta and cook until pasta and potatoes are tender, 7–10 minutes. Taste and correct seasonings, adding salt or pepper as needed. If soup is too thick, add water to thin.

BEEF AND BISCUITS

As a teenager, one of my sons came home from a three-day "pioneer trek" with a love for Dinty Moore stew; it kept him well fueled while pushing handcarts for miles. I thought it could be improved with more veggies and a biscuit topping. Dinty Moore, like Betty Crocker, is a fictional food character. He was dreamed up by the Hormel Company back in 1935. You may also use a comparable generic brand of canned beef stew. This is by no means haute cuisine, but it's a hearty, pantry-ready alternative to fast-food drive-through.

1 38-oz. can Dinty Moore Beef Stew or similar brand
1 24-oz. can Dinty Moore Beef Stew or similar brand
1 C. frozen corn
1 C. frozen peas
1 C. canned, petite-diced tomatoes (if you like tomatoes, use the whole 14.5-oz. can)
1 tube of 8 jumbo-sized refrigerated biscuits (or 10 small biscuits)

1. Preheat oven to 400 degrees (or temperature specified on biscuit package).

2. Empty cans of stew into 9-by-13-inch microwavable casserole dish. Add corn, peas, and tomatoes, and gently stir until evenly mixed.

2. Place stew in microwave on high for about 10–15 minutes to heat through. Then place in the oven to finish cooking.

3. While stew is heating, place biscuits on greased 13-by-9-inch pan.

Bake biscuits in oven 8–10 minutes, or according to package directions, until golden brown.

5. When biscuits are golden and stew is bubbling, remove both from the oven. Scoop the biscuits off pan with a wide spatula and arrange on top of hot stew.

Option: You can make own drop-style biscuits as toppers, but refrigerated biscuits shave off time.

TERRIFIC TACO SOUP

Prep time: 30 minutes | Makes 6 1 1/2-cup servings

This is a pantry- and budget-friendly recipe for hungry families. Place tortilla chips in bowls, ladle the soup over them, and let everyone pile on their favorite toppings.

1 lb. lean ground beef
2 Tbsp. dried chopped onion
3 10-oz. cans diced tomatoes with mild green chiles (Ro-Tel)
2 15-oz. cans kidney, black, or pinto beans, drained and rinsed
1 14-oz. can corn, drained
2 14-oz. cans beef broth
1 1.25-oz. pkg. taco seasoning mix (about 1/4 C.)
Tortilla chips
Optional garnishes: hot sauce, grated cheese, low-fat sour cream, diced green onion, sliced black olives, guacamole, and tortilla chips.

1. In a large saucepan, sauté ground beef with onion flakes over medium heat until lightly browned. Break up beef into small pieces as it cooks.

3. Drain fat from ground beef if necessary.

4. Add tomatoes, beans, corn, beef broth, and seasoning mix. Simmer, covered, 15–20 minutes.

5. Place a handful of tortilla chips in each of six bowls. Ladle soup over top. Garnish with grated cheese, sour cream, chopped onion, cilantro, sliced black olives, or guacamole.

RJ'S STUFFED PEPPER SOUP

Prep time: 30 minutes | *Makes about 6 1-cup servings*

RJ's was an eatery near Kirtland, Ohio, that gained a following among tourists and missionaries from the Church of Jesus Christ of Latter-day Saints during 2003–2010. Located near LDS Church history sites such as the Kirtland Temple, RJ's saw so many Utahns that it began offering Utah's traditional "fry sauce" along with its signature barbecue sauce. My son, Jess, savored an occasional pulled-pork sandwich there while serving in the Ohio Cleveland Mission. My cousin, Carol Cluff, also a former missionary and RJ's fan, shared with me a recipe for the restaurant's signature Stuffed Pepper Soup. Since it was a flexible type of recipe, open to some "guesstimates" and individual tweaking, I streamlined it with quick-cook brown rice, frozen peppers, and dried onion flakes. Owner Tom Ponzurick gave me permission to run the recipe as a nostalgic tribute to RJ's—closed, but not forgotten.

1. Sauté ground beef, onion, and chopped peppers in a 4-to-6-quart stockpot over medium-high heat until beef is browned.

2. Add remaining ingredients and simmer 15–20 minutes until cooked. Taste and adjust seasonings before serving.

1 lb. lean ground beef
2 Tbsp. minced dry onion (or 1/2 C. fresh chopped onion)
2 C. frozen chopped green pepper (or 1 green pepper and 1 red pepper, chopped)
2 10 3/4-oz. cans condensed tomato soup
2 14-oz. cans beef broth (or 4 beef bouillon cubes and 3 3/4 C. water)
1 14.5-oz. can petite-diced tomatoes
2 to 3 C. water
3/4 C. quick-cooking brown rice (such as Minute Rice)
1 tsp. garlic powder
Salt and pepper to taste
1 Tbsp. honey

ROOTIN' TOOTIN' CINCINNATI CHILI

Prep time: 45 minutes | Makes about 6 servings, with about 3/4 cup chili, 1/2 cup pasta, 1/3 cup beans

Cincinnati Chili is a regional style of chili known for unusual flavorings such as cinnamon, cloves, allspice, and chocolate; and the absence of chile peppers or powder. It is served over spaghetti noodles and topped with beans, cheese, or onions, which are referred to as "two-way," "three-way," "four-way," and "five-way." In this recipe, a can of root beer adds some of the sweet, spicy notes.

1 lb. ground beef
1 C. frozen chopped green pepper, or
    1 medium green pepper, chopped
3 Tbsp. dried chopped onion
1 Tbsp. garlic powder
1 14.5-oz. can petite-diced tomatoes,
    undrained
1 6-oz. can tomato paste
12-oz. can or bottle of root beer
    (Barq's or another less-sweet
    type)
1 Tbsp. chili powder
1 Tbsp. ground cumin
1 beef bouillon cube (or 1 tsp. beef
    base)
1 bay leaf
2 Tbsp. Worcestershire sauce
1 tsp. cinnamon
Optional flavorings: 2 tsp.
    unsweetened cocoa powder, pinch
    of allspice, cloves, or cayenne
    pepper
1 lb. spaghetti noodles
Options: Shredded cheddar cheese,
    diced fresh onion, 2 cans of
    kidney beans

1. In a large sauté pan, cook beef over medium-high heat, stirring and breaking up clumps of beef.

2. Add green pepper and onion to beef and continue cook until ground beef is no longer pink. Drain fat if necessary.

3. Stir in garlic powder, diced tomatoes, tomato paste, root beer, chili powder, cumin, bouillon cube, bay leaf, Worcestershire sauce, cinnamon, and optional flavorings. Cook, uncovered, over medium-high heat for 15–20 minutes, stirring occasionally to keep mixture from sticking.

4. While beef mixture cooks, fill 4-quart pot halfway full with water. Cover and set over high heat until water begins boiling. Add spaghetti; turn heat to medium and cover.

5. Cook pasta for 9–10 minutes, or until al dente (tender but still a little chewy). Drain pasta.

6. Remove bay leaf from spaghetti before serving.

7. Serve chili over spaghetti noodles for a "two-way."

8. Three-way: Spaghetti topped with chili and shredded cheese.

9. Four-way: Spaghetti, chili, shredded cheese, and either diced onion or kidney beans.

10. Five-way: Spaghetti, chili, shredded cheese, diced onion, and beans.

SMOKY PORK CHILI VERDE

Prep time: 30 minutes | *Makes about 6 1 1/2-cup servings*

For several years I was a judge at the Utah State Chili Cook-Off, where contestants spent hours dicing meat and chopping fresh chiles. This recipe is no match for those entries, but it takes less than 30 minutes from start to finish. You can use leftover pork roast or pork chops if you have them on hand. Chipotle chiles (smoked jalapeños) give a hint of smokiness to this dish. Be careful when working with them so you don't get burned. Don't scratch your nose or rub your eyes, and wash your hands afterward!

2 17-oz. pkg. of cooked roast pork with gravy (or cooked pork roast or chops with drippings)

2 16-oz. jars salsa verde

2 7-oz. cans diced green chiles

2 Tbsp. garlic powder

2 14-oz. cans chicken broth (or 4 C. water plus 4 chicken bouillon cubes)

1/4 C. chopped cilantro

2 chipotle chiles from a can of chiles in adobo sauce, plus 2 tsp. of the adobo sauce in the can (more if you want more intense heat)

1/2 tsp. sugar

1. Place roast pork on a cutting board and dice into 1/2- to 1-inch pieces. Add to a stockpot along with gravy and turn heat to high.

2. Add salsa verde, chiles, garlic powder, and chicken broth.

3. While soup is heating, finely chop cilantro. Add to pot.

4. Mince chipotle chiles and add to pot along with adobo sauce and sugar. (Reserve the rest of the canned chiles for future use.) Be sure to wash your hands right after handling the chipotle.

5. Let mixture come to a gentle boil for about 5 minutes.

6. Serve garnished with additional cilantro or tortilla chips.

Option: If you have time, add fresh roasted chiles.

PASTA AND GROUND BEEF SOUP

Prep time: 30 minutes | *Makes about 6 1 1/2-cup servings*

This soup is a fast fix, because ground beef cooks so quickly. Frozen onions, corn, and peas cut down prep time. Use extra-lean ground beef to skip the messy job of draining the fat.

1/2 lb. extra-lean ground beef
1 1/2 C. frozen onion (or 1/4 C. dried chopped onion)
1 C. frozen or canned corn
1 1/2 C. frozen carrots (or 1 1/4 C. sliced fresh carrots)
8 beef bouillon cubes
6 C. water
1 Tbsp. soy sauce
1 14.5-oz. can petite-diced tomatoes
2 C. rotini pasta or broken-up spaghetti noodles
1 C. frozen peas
Freshly ground pepper to taste
Salt to taste

1. In a 4-to-6-quart stockpot on medium-high heat, cook ground beef with onion, breaking beef into small clumps, about 5 minutes.

2. When beef is no longer pink, add corn, carrots, bouillon, water, soy sauce, and tomatoes; bring to a gentle boil.

3. Add pasta and cook 10 more minutes or until pasta is tender. Add frozen peas and remove from heat.

4. Add a few grinds of pepper. Taste and add more salt or pepper if needed.

ITALIAN WEDDING SOUP

Prep time: 25 minutes | Makes about 6 1 1/2 cup servings

This is called wedding soup because of the perfect marriage between the meatballs and the greens. You can use kale or escarole, but spinach is so easy. The meatballs are usually the time-consuming part of the soup; by buying premade, frozen meatballs you can skip this step. I used Italian-style turkey meatballs in my grocery store's freezer case; I'm sure pork or beef meatballs would also be delicious. Pesto adds a quick boost of flavor.

1. In a large pot, bring broth and onion to a boil.

2. Add pasta and cook 10 minutes.

3. While pasta cooks, pile spinach on a cutting board. Slice spinach into thin ribbons.

4. When pasta is almost tender, add meatballs. Allow soup to come back to a boil to heat meatballs completely, about 10 minutes.

5. Remove soup from heat and stir in pesto and spinach leaves. Add pepper to taste.

4 14-oz. cans chicken broth
2 Tbsp. dried onion
2 C. bowtie pasta
1 24-oz. pkg. frozen Italian-style meatballs
1/4 C. refrigerated pesto
2 C. spinach leaves, loosely packed
Several grinds of fresh pepper

QUICK TAILGATE CHILI

Prep time: 30 minutes | *Makes about 6 1 1/2-cup servings*

This Super Bowl–worthy recipe comes together within thirty minutes, and you don't have to peel, chop, or mince anything! Let everyone add their favorite toppings as desired.

1 lb. ground beef, 85 to 93 percent lean
1 Tbsp. dried chopped onion
1 7-oz. can chopped green chiles
1 16-oz. jar salsa
1 10-oz. can Ro-Tel diced tomatoes and chiles
1 Tbsp. dried cumin
1 tsp. garlic powder
1 6-oz. can tomato paste
1 C. water
1/2 tsp. salt, or to taste
3 15-oz. cans red beans
1 14-oz. can beef broth
1 14.5-oz. can petite-diced tomatoes
Garnishes: Tortilla chips, sour cream, chopped cilantro, chopped tomatoes, chopped avocado

1. In a large stockpot, brown ground beef, breaking into small chunks with spatula or fork.

2. Add remaining ingredients and stir until well mixed. Simmer 20–25 minutes.

3. Serve with tortilla chips, sour cream, chopped cilantro, chopped tomatoes, chopped avocado, and shredded cheese.

Options: For a smoky touch, add 2 chipotle chiles canned in adobo sauce plus 1 Tbsp. of the sauce. You can also add fresh roasted chiles.

OLD-FASHIONED VEGETABLE BEEF SOUP

Prep time: 1 hour, 15 minutes, Active prep time: 30 minutes | *Makes about 7 1 1/2-cup servings*

Most beef stew recipes take two or more hours to cook. We're saving some time by using precut stew meat. Quickly brown the beef, then add the broth so the beef can simmer and tenderize while you cut up the vegetables. This savory soup keeps on low heat for several hours. Make a batch on Saturday morning, set it on the back burner, and family members can help themselves to a bowl or two throughout the day.

1 Tbsp. vegetable oil
1 lb. of beef stew meat cubes
5 C. water
2 C. baby carrots
1/4 C. dried minced onion
7 beef bouillon cubes
1 C. sliced celery
2 medium potatoes, peeled and diced in 1-inch cubes (about 3 C.)
1 tsp. garlic powder
1 tsp. dried thyme
2 bay leaves
1 14.5-oz. can diced tomatoes
1 tsp. freshly ground pepper
1 C. corn kernels, canned or frozen
1 C. frozen peas
Options: 1/2 C. chopped red or green pepper, 1 C. frozen green beans, 2 Tbsp. chopped parsley

1. Heat oil in 6-quart stockpot over high heat. Cook beef so it's browned on all sides, about 5 minutes. Add water, carrots, onion, and bouillon cubes. Bring soup to a gentle boil.

2. While beef is cooking, slice celery and add to pot.

3. Peel and dice potatoes and add to pot along with garlic, thyme, bay leaves, tomatoes, pepper, and corn.

4. Keep soup at a gentle boil for at least 30 minutes, or until meat and vegetables are tender.

5. Taste and correct seasonings (you may want more garlic, bouillon, thyme, or pepper, depending on individual taste).

6. Add peas during the last few minutes of cooking so they don't lose their bright color.

Slow cooker method: Place the beef in slow cooker on high, with 1 C. of water and 7 beef bouillon cubes. Cook for at least one hour. While beef is cooking, prep vegetables. After beef has cooked for one hour, add 5 C. water and all the ingredients except frozen peas. Cook on high for 3 more hours or on low for 5–6 hours. Add peas a few minutes before serving.

BEEF STROGANOFF SOUP

Prep time: 25 minutes | *Makes about 6 1 1/2-cup servings*

This is a great way to use leftover roast beef from Sunday dinner.

1 Tbsp. oil

12-oz. pkg. mirepoix blend (or 2/3 C. fresh chopped onion, 1/3 C. sliced celery, and 1/3 C. chopped carrots)

2 Tbsp. dried chopped onion

1 8-oz. pkg. sliced fresh mushrooms

7 beef bouillon cubes

7 C. water

1 1/2 C. dry rotini pasta

3 C. cooked roast beef, cubed

1 tsp. garlic powder

1/2 tsp. thyme

1 tsp. pepper

1 C. sour cream (can be light sour cream)

1. Heat oil over medium-high heat and add mirepoix blend, onion, and mushrooms. Stir and cook for 5 minutes until vegetables are limp.

2. Add bouillon cubes, water, and pasta, and cook for 10 minutes at a gentle boil.

3. While the pasta cooks, place the roast beef on a cutting board and dice into cubes. Add to the pot.

4. Add garlic, thyme, and pepper.

5. When pasta is thoroughly cooked, stir in sour cream.

ROOT BEER-BRAISED BEEF STEW

Prep time: 10 minutes, Total cooking time: About 4 hours | Makes about 6 1 1/2-cup servings

This is a great Sunday meal. Take a few minutes to assemble it in the oven before you head out to your church services. A few hours later, you'll come home to tender beef chunks in a subtly sweet, spicy sauce, thanks to the root beer. By using the smallest red new potatoes, a package of baby carrots, and presliced mushrooms, you can skip any peeling and slicing.

1. Place stew meat, onions, potatoes, carrots, and mushrooms in a 4-to-6-quart ovenproof roasting pan or pot with a well-fitted lid.

2. In a bowl, mix root beer with bouillon granules, tomato paste, soy sauce, flour, and pepper. Pour over top of meat and vegetables.

3. Add bay leaves and cover pot with lid and place on middle rack of oven at 325 degrees. Cook for 3–4 hours, until beef is tender.

4. Remove pot from oven and gently stir veggies and meat so they are evenly coated with sauce. Taste and add additional salt or pepper, if needed, before serving.

2 lbs. beef stew meat, in chunks
1/4 C. dried chopped onion
1 1/2 lbs. small red potatoes, 1–2 inches in diameter
1 lb. baby carrots
1 C. sliced fresh mushrooms
12 oz. root beer (if you can only find a 20-oz. bottle, drink the remaining 8 oz.)
2 Tbsp. beef bouillon granules (or 6 beef bouillon cubes)
1 6-oz. can tomato paste
1 Tbsp. soy sauce
1 Tbsp. flour
Several grinds of pepper
2 bay leaves

SLOW COOKER SMOKY
NO-BEAN CHILI

Prep time: 3–4 hours or 6–8 hours | Makes about 6 1 1/2-cup servings

The International Chili Society, based in Terlingua, Texas, contends that "real chili" doesn't contain beans. While the rest of the country may not agree, the ICS doesn't allow beans in its legendary chili cookoffs. Robb Walsh, author of The Tex Mex Cookbook, claims that Texas-style chili con carne came from the Canary Island immigrants who settled San Antonio. The Canary Island women made a stew with meat, cumin, garlic, chile peppers, and wild onion—and no beans. To bean or not to bean? That's your choice. The smoky flavor comes from smoked paprika and chipotle chiles (smoked jalapeños). If you don't have smoked paprika, regular paprika can be used. Chipotles can be bought dried or in a small can with adobo sauce. I used two canned chipotles and saved the rest in the freezer for a future recipe. You can use 1–2 teaspoons of chipotle powder instead. Since preferences for heat and spice can vary, I suggest following the recipe then adding a few more chiles to taste. It's easier to add more heat than to subtract it.

2 canned chipotle chiles, with 1 Tbsp.
    of the adobo sauce (more if you
    want more heat)
2 lbs. beef stew meat, in cubes
2 14.5-oz. cans petite-diced tomatoes
2 7-oz. cans diced mild green chiles
1 tsp. smoked paprika
1 can beef broth
1 Tbsp. cumin
1 tsp. sugar
1 tsp. salt
1 C. tortilla chips, crushed
Sour cream, tortilla chips, cilantro,
    olives, salsa for garnish

1. With tongs, place chipotle chiles in a 1/4 C. measuring cup. Using kitchen shears, snip chiles into small ribbons.

2. Place chiles and all other ingredients except tortilla chips and salt in a slow cooker. Cook on low heat 6–8 hours or on high heat 5–6 hours.

3. Stir in tortilla chips during last half hour of cooking. Taste and add more salt if desired.

4. Serve with sour cream, tortilla chips, cilantro, olives, and salsa.

PEPPERONI SOUPREME

Prep time: 30 minutes | *Makes 6 1 1/2-cup servings*

This hearty soup makes you think of a crustless pizza in a bowl. Frozen veggies and jarred pizza sauce make it simple to prepare. Serve with a crisp green salad, and dinner is ready.

1 1/2 C. frozen onion (about 1 C. fresh)

1 C. frozen green pepper (or 1 small green pepper)

2 14-oz. cans chicken broth

2 C. bowtie pasta

2 C. chopped pepperoni

1 7-oz. can mushrooms

1/2 tsp. crushed red pepper (more if desired)

2 tsp. Italian seasoning

1 tsp. sugar

2 14-oz. jars pizza sauce

1 C. water

1 C. milk or half-and-half

1 C. shredded mozzarella

1. In a 4- to 6-quart nonstick stockpot, cook frozen onion and green pepper over high heat until limp.

2. Add chicken broth and bowtie pasta and let mixture come to a gentle boil. Cook for 5 minutes.

3. While soup is cooking, chop pepperoni, if necessary. Add to soup with mushrooms, crushed red pepper, Italian seasoning, sugar, and pizza sauce, using the 1 C. of water to rinse the last of sauce from the jar.

4. Let soup boil gently until pasta is tender. Stir in milk. Taste and adjust seasonings. Serve with a heaping spoonful of mozzarella cheese.

SAVORY SAUSAGE TORTELLINI SOUP

Prep time: 30 minutes | Makes 6 1-1/2-cup servings

By using frozen onions, peppers, and presliced mushrooms, you don't need to do any prep work for this spicy soup. My heat-seeking son loved the flavor of hot sausage in this soup, but my other tasters found it too fiery. If you use mild sausage, you can always bump up the heat by increasing the amount of crushed red pepper.

1 lb. bulk sausage
1 C. chopped frozen green pepper
2 C. chopped frozen onion
1 C. sliced fresh mushrooms (or 1 small can mushroom stems and pieces)
1 9–oz. pkg. refrigerated cheese tortellini
2 14-oz. cans beef broth
1 26-oz. jar spaghetti sauce
1/2 tsp. crushed red pepper
1 tsp. garlic
1/2 C. half-and-half, optional
1/4 C. Parmesan or mozzarella cheese

1. In a 4-to-6-quart stockpot, brown sausage over medium heat, about 5 minutes.

2. Add green pepper, onion, and mushrooms, and continue to cook, stirring, until vegetables are limp, about 5 minutes.

3. Add tortellini, broth, spaghetti sauce, crushed red pepper, and garlic. Bring mixture to a gentle boil and cook 7–8 minutes or until tortellini are tender. Add half-and-half, if desired.

4. Serve each bowl with a sprinkle of Parmesan or mozzarella.

PRESTO ZUPPA TOSCANA

Prep time: 30 minutes | Makes about 6 1 1/2-cup servings

Inspired by Olive Garden's Zuppa Toscana, this creamy sausage soup saves time with hash browns potatoes O'Brien and packaged bacon pieces.

1. Place sausage in a 4-to-6-quart stockpot and brown it over medium-high heat, breaking into small pieces as it cooks.

2. Drain fat from sausage.

3. Add potatoes, broth, water, garlic, onion, red pepper flakes, and bacon pieces. Cook at a gentle boil about 5 minutes.

4. While soup is cooking, chop kale or Swiss chard. Add to soup and cook an additional 10 minutes or until kale and potatoes are tender.

5. Turn off heat and stir in cream and mix until well blended.

1 lb. bulk Italian sausage
1 28-oz. bag hash brown potatoes O'Brien
3 14-oz. cans chicken broth
1 C. water
2 tsp. garlic powder
3 Tbsp. dried minced onion
1/2 tsp. crushed red pepper flakes (more if you like spicy heat)
1/2 C. packaged real bacon pieces
4 C. chopped kale or Swiss chard, loosely packed
1 C. whipping cream

BEEF BORSCHT

Prep time: 40 minutes | *Makes about 4 1 1/2-cup servings*

This recipe was inspired by a visit with Masha Kirilenko, wife of former Utah Jazz forward Andrei Kirilenko. While working at the Deseret News, I visited their home the day after Andrei broke his wrist during a game, and Masha cooked him one of his favorite soups, beef borscht. This was Russian comfort food at its best. Masha told me, "You have to be born and raised in Russia to like borscht." But her rich, flavorful addition of filet mignon chunks could have won over some Americans. "It's a very expensive borscht," she noted when she shared her recipe with the Deseret News. My version uses the more economical stir-fry steak strips instead of filet mignon. It also speeds things up with diced tomatoes, bagged pre-cut carrots and frozen onions.

4 medium-size new red potatoes
   (also known as boiling potatoes),
   peeled and halved
1 Tbsp. vegetable oil
1 1/2 cups frozen chopped onions
2 14-oz. cans beef broth
1/2 stir-fry beef steak strips
1 1/2 cups chopped baby carrots
5-6 medium-size fresh beets, sliced
1 14.5-oz. can diced tomatoes
Salt and freshly ground black pepper
3/4 C. sour cream
1 Tbsp. fresh dill

1. Place the potatoes in a medium-size pot. Cover with water and bring to a boil. Cook until potatoes are tender. Drain and cover to keep warm.

2. While potatoes are boiling, heat oil in a 3-quart heavy saucepan over low heat. Add the beef and onions, and cook, stirring frequently, until beef is browned.

3. Add broth, and bring soup to a gentle boil.

4. While soup is heating, coarsely chop the carrots and beets and add them to the pot with the tomatoes. Add salt and pepper to taste.

5. Simmer, covered, until beef and vegetables are tender (about 20 minutes). Ladle borscht into four bowls and divide the potatoes among the bowls.

6. Top with sour cream and sprinkle with dill.

HUNGARIAN GOULASH

Prep time: 10 minutes, Cooking time: 3 1/2 to 4 hours | *Makes 6 1 1/4-cup servings*

This is a longer-cooking stew, but it takes just a few minutes to assemble. For its rich flavor and color, Hungarian cooks rely on paprika and a seasoning blend called Vegeta. You may be able to order it online or find it at specialty stores. For simplicity, I chose to use Mrs. Dash Original seasoning, which contains many of the same ingredients. I'm also told the traditional cooking method is over a fire in a cast-iron pot. A cast-iron Dutch oven in a regular oven is the next-best shortcut. (Place it on a sturdy baking sheet for stability.) If you don't have a Dutch oven, you can cook it in a roasting pan or in your slow cooker.

1/3 C. sweet paprika
2 tsp. Vegeta or Mrs. Dash
1 tsp. salt
1 tsp. freshly ground pepper
2 Tbsp. tomato paste
1 can beef broth
2 lbs. boneless beef stew meat, already cubed
3 C. frozen chopped onion
3 medium russet potatoes, peeled and quartered
2 C. baby carrots
1 bay leaf

1. In a bowl, mix together paprika, seasonings, tomato paste, and beef broth.

2. Place stew meat, onion, potatoes, baby carrots, and bay leaf in a Dutch oven, or another ovenproof pan or pot with a tight-fitting lid.

3. Pour paprika mixture over top and toss to coat beef and vegetables.

4. Place the pan in oven at 300 degrees. Cook for 3 1/2–4 hours.

Option: If using a slow cooker, cook on high for 3 1/2–4 hours; or low 6–8 hours.

Bratten's Clam Chowder 74

Larry H. Miller's Seafood Gumbo 76

Golden Corn and Crab Chowder........................78

Rah-Rah! Ramen 79

Lobster Bisque 80

New Orleans Gumbo 82

Salmon Chowder..84

Kung Pao Shrimp Bowl....................................86

Manhattan Clam Chowder 87

Thai-Style Curry Shrimp Soup 88

Cioppino 90

SEAFOOD SOUPS

BRATTEN'S CLAM CHOWDER

Prep time: 30 minutes | Makes 6 1 1/2-cup servings

Bratten's Seafood Grottos were Utah hot spots in the 1970s, with several locations along the Wasatch Front. The clam chowder's following lasted long after the restaurants closed, and the recipe was passed around in many neighborhood cookbooks. I streamlined it with frozen diced potatoes and by microwaving the vegetables instead of simmering them on the stove. By the time you've made a roux, the vegetables are tender and ready to add to the soup. I also reduced the amount of butter. I tested the recipe using fat-free half-and-half, and it was still rich and creamy. Your waistline will thank you.

1 C. finely diced onion (or about 1 1/2 C. frozen diced onion)

1 C. finely diced celery (about 2 ribs)

3 C. frozen hash browns (or 2 C. diced raw potatoes)

2 6 1/2-oz. cans of minced clams

1 C. water

1/2 C. butter

1/2 C. flour

1 quart half-and-half cream (or fat-free half-and-half)

1 1/2 tsp. salt

Pepper to taste

1. Dice onion and slice celery. Place onion, celery, and hash browns in a microwavable casserole bowl.

2. Drain juice from clams and pour liquid over vegetables. Add 1 C. water.

3. Place a lid on bowl and microwave on high 10–12 minutes, stirring at the 5-minute point.

4. While clams and potatoes are cooking in microwave, melt butter over medium heat in a heavy stockpot. Make a roux by stirring flour and butter together with a wire whisk. Continue cooking and stirring roux for about 5 minutes.

5. Slowly add half-and-half while continuing to stir and cook over medium heat until mixture is thick and smooth.

6. Add cooked vegetables and clams. Allow soup to cook until potatoes and celery are tender.

7. Add salt and pepper to taste.

Option: Garnish with parsley and oyster crackers.

LARRY H. MILLER'S SEAFOOD GUMBO

Prep time: 45 minutes | *Makes 8 to 9 1 1/2-cup servings*

When the Utah Jazz wives published a cookbook, I was invited to Larry H. and Gail Miller's home where I met some of the wives and taste tested recipes. One of the book's recipes was Larry Miller's Seafood Gumbo. At the time, Gail showed me his handwritten recipe. After Larry passed away, Gail gave me permission to use the recipe in this book. If it were up to me, I would add the shrimp and scallops near the end of the cooking time so they don't become rubbery in texture. But, far be it from me to tinker with a signature Larry H. Miller dish! Except for a shorter simmering time, I kept the recipe "as is."

3 Tbsp. butter
2 diced onion
4–6 cloves garlic, finely chopped
6 C. chicken broth (or 6 chicken
    bouillon cubes and 6 C. water)
2 14 1/2-oz. cans stewed tomatoes
1 lb. medium-size peeled shrimp, tails
    off, cooked
1/2 to 3/4 lbs. scallops, cut in 1/2
    inch pieces, or bay scallops
1/2 to 3/4 lbs. sliced fresh or frozen
    okra
 2 tsp. salt
1/2 tsp. dried basil
2 bay leaves
1/4 tsp. red (cayenne) pepper
25 to 30 turns of freshly ground
    pepper
3 stalks chopped celery
 1/2 C. uncooked rice

1. Melt butter on low heat in a large, 4-quart soup pan while you chop onion and garlic.

2. Turn up heat and sauté onion and garlic until translucent, about 5 minutes.

3. Add chicken broth and all other ingredients except rice and celery.

4. Bring to a boil and simmer 15 minutes. Meanwhile, chop celery.

5. Add rice and celery. Cook 20–25 minutes, until rice and celery are tender.

GOLDEN CORN AND CRAB CHOWDER

Prep time: 30 minutes | *Makes 6 1-1/2-cup servings*

If you'd like a smoother texture, blend all three cans of corn. If you can afford fresh or frozen crabmeat, do it. You can also use shrimp instead of crab.

3 15-oz. cans corn, drained
2 Tbsp. dried chopped onion
2 14-oz. cans chicken broth or 3 1/2
    C. fish stock
3 C. frozen hash brown potatoes
    O'Brien
1 Tbsp. dried parsley flakes or chives
Salt to taste
2 tsp. Old Bay seasoning, or to taste
1 tsp. fresh ground pepper
1 tsp. lemon juice
1 tsp. sugar
2 Tbsp. cornstarch
1/4 C. water
3 6-oz. cans crab, not drained (or
    about 2 C. of lump crabmeat,
    picked through for shells)
1 C. half-and-half or milk

1. Pour 2 cans corn in blender with onion flakes and 1 can chicken broth (or 1 C. fish stock). Blend until smooth.

2. Drain third can of corn and add to a stockpot with pureed corn, remaining broth or stock, hash browns, parsley flakes, salt, Old Bay seasoning, freshly ground pepper, lemon juice, and sugar. Turn heat to high.

3. While mixture is coming to a boil, mix cornstarch and water until smooth. Add to soup and stir as soup gently boils and thickens, about 5 minutes. Add crab and crab liquid. Thoroughly mix in the half-and-half or milk. Serve with oyster crackers, if desired.

RAH-RAH! RAMEN

Prep time: 10 minutes | Makes 6 1 1/2-cup servings

The starving student standby gets a quick makeover with shrimp, crunchy pea pods, and peppers. If you're serving this to someone who is allergic to MSG, omit the seasoning packets and use no-MSG chicken broth instead.

On a cutting board, thinly slice pepper. Add to a large, microwavable bowl with ramen noodles, sauce packets, and water. Cover and microwave on high for about 5–6 minutes. Water should be boiling.

While noodles are boiling, slice pea pods in half on the diagonal.

Remove bowl of noodles from the microwave. Stir in pea pods, shrimp, mushrooms, and water chestnuts. Microwave 1 to 2 more minutes until soup is heated through.

1 large red or green bell pepper, thinly sliced

3 pkg. ramen noodles with chicken-flavored seasoning packet

7 C. water

1 C. Chinese pea pods, sliced diagonally in two

2 to 3 C. cooked and deveined shrimp (cocktail size or smaller, preferably with tails off)

1 can mushroom stems and pieces, drained

1 can water chestnuts, drained and rinsed, optional

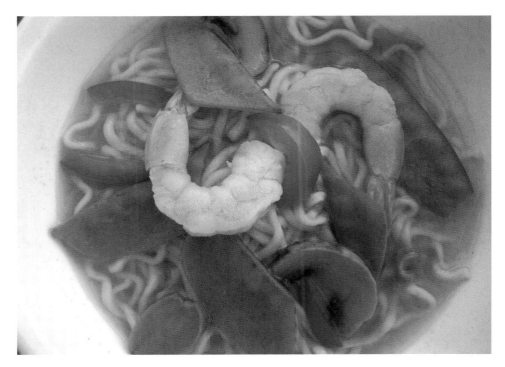

LOBSTER BISQUE

Prep time: 45 minutes | Makes 6 1 1/4-cup servings

This luxurious soup is a little more time-consuming than most of the recipes in this book. And unless you live in New England, it will likely cost more too. The first time I tried lobster bisque was at a restaurant in London. It was silky smooth, and I wondered where the lobster was. In his oh-so-very proper way, the waiter told me that the soup was flavored with lobster and its shell, but a true bisque is smooth, not chunky. A lot of recipes call for cooking live lobsters, extracting the meat, and either grinding the shells, sautéing the shells in oil, or flaming them with alcohol to extract their flavor. But Market Street Grill chef Ty Frederickson told me that their restaurant group's Seafood Combo Bisque doesn't use any shells. "The shell has more to do with getting the reddish color and not the flavor," he said. "It would probably take a whole day to grind down shells and make a paste of them." My shortcut involves two lobster tails, which are readily available frozen and easier to work with. Cooking the shell imparts a little flavor, but I found that adding 8 ounces of clam juice helped it along. And, despite the words of that waiter in London, I like having little chunks of lobster in my bisque. Many recipes call for sherry, brandy, wine, or other spirits. I added imitation brandy-flavored extract and a little white grape juice instead.

2 uncooked lobster tails, fresh or thawed if frozen (or 2 cooked lobster tails)
4 C. water
3 Tbsp. butter
1 12-oz. pkg. frozen mirepoix blend (or 2/3 C. fresh chopped onion, 1/3 C. sliced celery, and 1/3 C. chopped carrots)
2 Tbsp. flour
2 tsp. jarred minced garlic (or about 1/2 tsp. garlic powder)
8 oz. clam juice
1/4 C. tomato paste
1/2 C. white grape juice or apple juice
1 tsp. brandy extract (optional)
1 Tbsp. Worcestershire sauce
1 C. cream (or fat-free half-and-half)
Salt and pepper to taste

1. Place lobster tails in medium-size pot with water (enough to cover tails) and bring water to a boil. Let water gently boil for about 5 minutes, until shell is bright orange and lobster meat is opaque and cooked through. Don't overcook.

2. Meanwhile, heat butter in a stockpot over medium-high heat and add vegetables, stirring occasionally as they cook, about 5 minutes, until onion begins to turn golden.

3. Take lobster tails from cooking water and allow to cool for about 5–10 minutes.

4. While lobster cools, add flour to cooked vegetable mixture and stir until well blended, about 5 minutes. Stir in garlic, clam juice, tomato paste, white grape juice, brandy extract, and Worcestershire sauce. Let mixture simmer about 10 minutes.

5. While mixture simmers, use a sharp paring knife to make a slit down the inside center of each lobster tail shell and push it open to get to lobster meat. With your fingers, pull out lobster meat and place on a cutting board.

6. Place pieces of lobster shell back in cooking water and bring water to a gentle boil. Let it boil for 10 minutes.

7. While lobster shells are boiling and soup mixture is simmering, chop lobster meat into small chunks. You should have about 1 C. of lobster meat.

8. Strain lobster shell water through a sieve into the stockpot and stir until well mixed with soup mixture. Remove soup from heat.

9. Pull off any remaining lobster meat sticking to shells and add to tail meat reserved on cutting board. Discard shells.

10. In two batches, puree soup mixture in a blender. Or using a handheld blender, whisk until mixture is smooth.

11. Stir in cream and about half of lobster chunks. Use rest of lobster chunks as a garnish when serving.

Options: You can use shrimp or crab instead of lobster, or a combination of the three for a seafood bisque.

NEW ORLEANS GUMBO

Prep time: 45 minutes | *Makes 8–10 1 1/2-cup servings*

Gumbo is a hearty stew that can stretch to feed a crowd, and it tastes even better the second day, according to Poppy Tooker, the New Orleans cooking teacher who beat chef Bobby Flay in a Food Network gumbo throw-down. I attended one of her gumbo-making demonstrations at the New Orleans Cooking School in 2008. Gumbo usually contains some type of seafood, poultry, or small game, and spicy sausage. The biggest time challenge is making the roux that thickens and flavors the gumbo. Some recipes specify cooking this mixture of oil and flour for forty to sixty minutes, until it turns a deep brown color. But it burns easily if you get impatient and turn the heat too high or forget to stir it. I've found that you can brown the roux in about ten to fifteen minutes if you're constantly stirring over medium-high heat. It helps to let the oil warm up on low heat while you're chopping the vegetables.
Many gumbo recipes call for frying the okra and sausage separately before adding them to the gumbo.
I shaved time by using frozen okra and letting both the sausage and okra cook in the gumbo.

1/2 C. vegetable oil
1 1/2 C. frozen chopped onion (or 1 onion, chopped)
1 1/2 C. celery, chopped (about 3 stalks)
1 1/2 C. frozen bell pepper (or 1 green bell pepper, chopped)
1 C. flour
1 14.5-oz. can petite-diced tomatoes
1 lb. frozen okra, thinly sliced
2 Tbsp. dried thyme
1 bay leaf
7 C. stock (can be chicken broth, clam juice, or a combination of both)
1/2 lb. smoked sausage (andouille or kielbasa)
2 C. chopped chicken breast or thighs
1 clove garlic, chopped
Salt and pepper
2 C. uncooked rice
4 1/4 C. water

1. Place 1/2 C. of the oil in a 4- to 6-quart stockpot over low heat.

2. While oil heats, chop onion, celery, and bell pepper.

3. Turn up heat on oil and stir in flour, working out any lumps.

4. Keep stirring until mixture is almost as tan as a brown paper bag. The roux will thin as it cooks; if it begins to smoke, remove it from heat and stir constantly to cool slightly. Don't get distracted! If the phone or doorbell rings, ignore it or turn off heat.

5. Stir in onion, celery, and bell pepper. Sauté in roux for five minutes, then add tomatoes, okra, herbs, and stock.

6. Add sausage, chicken, and crab. Chop garlic and add it, along with salt and pepper to taste.

7. Simmer 10–15 minutes, stirring occasionally to be sure there's no sticking on the bottom.

8. While gumbo simmers, add rice and 4 1/4 C. water to a large glass casserole dish with a lid. Microwave on high, covered, for 5 minutes. Reduce power to medium-low (3 or 4 setting) and continue cooking, uncovered, for 15 more minutes, or until tender.

Any or all of the following seafood:

1 lb. shrimp, preferably raw and tails off

1/2 lb. crabmeat (or gumbo crabs if you can find them)

2 C. fresh oysters (or canned if fresh are unavailable)

1 bunch green onion, thinly sliced

Hot sauce, optional

Sprinkle of file powder, optional

9. Five minutes before serving, add raw or cooked shrimp, crab, oysters, and green onion, if using. Simmer five minutes. Serve over rice with hot sauce and a sprinkle of file powder stirred in, if desired.

SALMON CHOWDER

Prep time: 30 minutes | Makes 6 1 1/2-cup servings

This creamy chowder is perfect for a cold winter evening. Frozen diced potatoes and dried onion flakes mean there's no chopping necessary. I prefer using frozen or fresh salmon because of its bright color, but you can use canned salmon if desired.

2 14-oz. cans chicken broth (or fish stock or clam juice, if desired)
1 28-oz. pkg. O'Brien-style diced hash brown potatoes, with no added fat
1 15-oz. can corn
1 Tbsp. dried chopped onion
1/2 to 1 lb. fresh or frozen salmon fillets (or 2 6-oz. cans or pouches salmon)
2 Tbsp. cornstarch
1/4 C. water
1 8-oz. pkg. cream cheese or reduced-fat cream cheese
Chopped parsley if desired, for garnish
1 tsp. freshly ground pepper
1–2 tsp. lemon juice

1. Place broth, potatoes, corn, and onion flakes in large pot over high heat.

2. Bring soup to a gentle boil. Cook about 10 minutes or until potatoes are tender.

3. While soup is cooking, dice salmon into 1-inch pieces (or open canned salmon and drain). Cut cream cheese into chunks.

4. Mix cornstarch and water to a smooth paste. Stir cornstarch mixture into the boiling soup, and continue stirring until mixture thickens.

5. Mix cream cheese chunks into the soup, allowing cheese to melt and incorporate into the soup.

6. Add salmon chunks. Cook about 2 minutes, or until the salmon is opaque.

7. Add parsley, pepper, and lemon juice if desired. Taste and adjust seasonings as desired.

Options: You can add shrimp, crab, scallops, or other seafood.

KUNG PAO SHRIMP BOWL

Prep time: 30 minutes | Makes about 6 1 1/2-cup servings

This hot, spicy riff on a Chinese favorite saves time by using dried ground ginger instead of peeling and grating fresh ginger. Peeled, tail-off shrimp may be hard to find; you can also use cooked shrimp, but take care to just heat it through instead of overcooking it.

1 Tbsp. canola oil or peanut oil
1 bunch of green onions
1 rib celery, thinly sliced (about 3/4 C.)
1 red bell pepper, chopped (about 1 C.)
1/2 C. teriyaki sauce/marinade
2 tsp. dried ground ginger
1 Tbsp. garlic powder
1 tsp. crushed red pepper (more if you
    want it super spicy)
1 tsp. rice or apple cider vinegar
3 14-oz. cans chicken broth
4 oz. (1/4 of a 1-lb. pkg.) dry spaghetti
1 32-oz. pkg. large raw shrimp, tail off
    (you may also use cooked shrimp,
    if necessary)
1/2 C. chopped dry-roasted peanuts

1. Heat the oil over low heat in a 4-to-6-quart quart stockpot while you slice onion in half-inch slices. Reserve 1/2 C. of green parts. Then slice celery and bell pepper.

2. Turn heat to high and sauté white parts of onions, along with celery and bell pepper, stirring about 5 minutes, or until limp.

3. Add teriyaki sauce, ginger, garlic powder, crushed red pepper, vinegar, and broth, and bring to a gentle boil.

4. Break spaghetti in half lengthwise and stir into broth. Cook about 5 minutes, until spaghetti is almost al dente.

5. Add shrimp. Stir and cook until shrimp are barely pink, about 5 minutes.

6. Stir in green onion. Serve each bowl topped with a spoonful of peanuts.

MANHATTAN CLAM CHOWDER

Prep time: 30 minutes | Makes about 6 1 1/2-cup servings

Also known as "red" clam chowder, this soup uses a tomato base instead of cream or milk. Frozen vegetables, canned clams, and tomatoes bring the soup together quickly. Bottled clam juice adds to the briny flavor.

1. In a nonstick 4-to-6-quart stockpot, heat oil over high heat. Sauté mirepoix vegetables and bell pepper about 5 minutes.

2. Add chopped clams with their juice, potatoes, bacon, garlic, onion, bay leaves, oregano, thyme, red pepper, clam juice, tomatoes, and chicken stock. Bring to a gentle boil and cook 15 minutes, or until potatoes are tender.

3. While potatoes are cooking, place parsley in a measuring cup and snip with kitchen shears until minced. Add to the soup. Season with salt and pepper to taste.

4. Turn off heat and allow soup to sit another 5 minutes to allow flavors to blend before serving.

1 Tbsp. canola oil
1 pkg. frozen mirepoix blend (or 2/3 C. fresh chopped onion, 1/3 C. sliced celery and 1/3 C. chopped carrot)
1/2 C. frozen bell pepper
3 6 1/2-oz. cans of chopped clams with their juice
5 C. frozen hash brown potatoes
1/2 C. packaged real bacon bits
2 tsp. garlic powder
1 Tbsp. dried onion flakes
3 bay leaves
1/2 tsp. oregano
1/2 tsp. thyme
1/4 to 1/2 tsp. crushed red pepper flakes (use more if you want more heat)
2 bottles clam juice
2 14.5-oz. cans petite-diced tomatoes
1 can chicken stock
3 Tbsp. chopped fresh parsley (or 1 Tbsp. dried minced parsley)
Freshly ground salt and pepper to taste

THAI-STYLE SHRIMP CURRY SOUP

Prep time: 25 minutes | Makes 6 1 1/2-cup servings

This is simple to make thanks to ready-prepared red curry simmer sauce, found in the Asian section of grocery stores. I use Thai Kitchen brand. The matchstick carrots and sugar snap peas add color and crunch. This is mild flavored as far as curries go. If you want more heat, add a half teaspoon of red pepper flakes (or more). Also if you want more lemon grass flavor, try adding a tablespoon of fresh crushed lemon grass in a tube, Gourmet Garden or Marvini brands.

2 Tbsp. oil
1 C. frozen onion
1 C. mushrooms, sliced
2 C. matchstick carrots (or shred your own or used sliced)
1 red pepper, cut in thin strips
2 11.09-oz. jars red curry simmering sauce (such as Thai Kitchen brand)
1 tsp. ginger
1 14 oz. can chicken broth
1/4 C. chopped cilantro, divided
1 C. fresh sugar snap peas
4 C. frozen, cooked, tail-off shrimp

Heat oil in a 4-to-6-quart stockpot over medium-high heat. Add onion, mushrooms, and carrots, and cook about 5 minutes.

2. Meanwhile, cut red pepper into thin strips. Add to pot to cook, stirring, about 5 more minutes, until vegetables are limp and fragrant.

3. Add red curry simmering sauce to pot. Stir to mix well. Add ginger and chicken stock. Simmer 5–10 minutes.

4. While soup is simmering, place cilantro in a measuring cup and snip with kitchen shears until well chopped. Add half of cilantro to pot and continue simmering a few more minutes.

 4. Stir in sugar snap peas and shrimp. Cook 1–2 minutes and then remove the soup from the heat. Allow the soup to sit a few minutes so the shrimp is heated through. Top each bowl with a sprinkle of cilantro.

Option: Fresh green beans can be used instead of sugar snap peas. Add them while the soup is simmering, allowing them about 5 minutes to become crisp-tender.

CIOPPINO

Prep time: 30 minutes | Makes about 6 1 1/2-cup servings

This San Francisco tomatoey seafood stew has roots in Italian fishing communities. It was among the first dishes served along the city's Fisherman's Wharf. Historically the recipe varied with the daily catch. Clams or mussel shells in the broth give it that signature look, and Dungeness crabs make it authentic to the Pacific Northwest. If you live in a landlocked area, you are limited on price and availability. I found live mussels at my grocer's seafood department and relied on canned clams, lump crabmeat, and shrimp for the rest. If you're able to find more shellfish, go for it. If you can't find uncooked shrimp, use ready-cooked, but don't add it until the very end of cooking time so it doesn't turn rubbery. Just remember that eating shellfish swimming in red broth can be messy. Offer thick-sliced bread (such as sourdough) to soak up the broth, use a lot of napkins, and wear dark colors!

1 lb. mussels
2 Tbsp. olive oil
2 C. frozen onion
1 14.5-oz. can petite-diced tomatoes
1/2 tsp. thyme
2 Tbsp. garlic powder
1 tsp. oregano
1/2 tsp. red pepper flakes (add more if desired)
1 8-oz. bottle clam juice
1/2 to 1 lb. white fish (cod, tilapia)
1 can clams with juice
1 lb. large shrimp
1 lb. mussels
1 lb. white fish (tilapia in this case)
1/2 lb. bay scallops (optional)
1/2 lb. lump crabmeat, optional

1. Bring 2 C. of water to boil in a saucepan. While water is heating, rinse mussels and debeard them if necessary (cut off little beard-like thing protruding from between the shell. Luckily, most farmed mussels don't have beards.)

2. Add mussels to boiling water and cook for 3–4 minutes until shells open. Turn off heat and let them sit in cooking water.

3. While mussels are cooking, heat oil in a 4-to-6-quart stockpot over high heat. Sauté the onion until softened, about 5 minutes. Stir in tomatoes, thyme, garlic, oregano, red pepper flakes, and clam juice. Bring to a boil.

4. While broth is cooking, dice fish into 1-inch pieces. Reserve.

5. Strain mussel cooking water through a sieve to remove any sediment and add it to pot. Let broth come to a gentle boil for 5 minutes.

6. If using canned clams, add along with scallops, crabmeat, fish, and shrimp, if using raw shrimp. Cook 5–10 minutes, until fish is opaque.

7. If using cooked shrimp, add just a few minutes before serving and cook just until heated through. Add mussels to pot just before serving. Divide mussels and seafood equally among six bowls.

Broccoli Cheddar Soup 94

Loaded Potato Soup..96

Creamy Tomato Tortellini Soup.................................98

Minestrone 100

Minted Pea Soup...101

Biggest Loser Resort's Roasted Red Pepper Bisque 102

Maple-Kissed Butternut Squash Bisque..................104

Creamy Cauliflower Soup 106

Cheesy Veggie Chowder..108

Quick Vegetarian Veggie Soup.................................110

Curried Carrot Bisque...111

Cream of Asparagus Soup 112

Fennel Bisque 114

French Onion Soup with Parmesan Croutons.........116

Zucchini and Bacon Soup 118

Gazpacho...119

Garden Tomato Bisque..120

Harvest Pumpkin Soup with Cheddar 122

Mega-Mushroom Soup...124

Roasted Garlic Bisque 126

Garden Vegetable Soup 128

Easy Cheesy Potato-Broccoli Soup 129

Silken Potato Leek Soup 130

Rosemary Potato and Corn Chowder 132

Rich Mushroom and Brown Rice Soup 134

Hotel Utah Borscht...136

VEGETABLE SOUPS

BROCCOLI CHEDDAR SOUP

Prep time: 30 minutes | *Makes about 6 1 1/2-cup servings*

My introduction to this soup in the early 1980s was in Hong Kong, of all places. It was on the menu of our hotel's restaurant. I asked the manager for the recipe, and a couple of months later, the chef's recipe arrived at our address in Saudi Arabia. It called for peeling and chopping fresh onions and broccoli. Since I was living in an area where fresh vegetables were costly and not always available, I streamlined it with frozen broccoli and dried onion flakes. Because it's so convenient, I've been making it that way ever since.

3 Tbsp. butter
3 Tbsp. all-purpose flour
2 cans chicken or vegetable stock
2 C. milk or half-and-half
1/3 C. dried chopped onion
2 12-oz. pkg. frozen chopped broccoli,
    or broccoli cuts, thawed
2 cups shredded sharp cheddar cheese
Salt and grinds of fresh pepper to
    taste
Pinch ground nutmeg
1/2 C. Parmesan cheese or sour cream,
    for garnish

1. Melt butter over medium heat in a 4- to 6-quart stockpot.

2. Sprinkle with flour and cook, stirring, for about 2 minutes, to make a roux.

3. Add stock, milk, dried onion, and broccoli, and stir well. Turn up heat and allow mixture to come to a boil, stirring occasionally.

4. Reduce heat to medium-low and let mixture to cook until broccoli is tender, about 10 minutes, stirring occasionally. Remove from heat and allow to cool a few minutes. Puree until smooth in two batches in a stand blender or with a hand-held blender.

5. Return to pot and add cheddar, stirring until cheese is melted. Add salt, pepper, and nutmeg to taste.

6. Ladle into heated bowls and garnish with a heaping Tbsp. of Parmesan or sour cream, if desired.

Options: If you have time, you can use about 4 C. of chopped fresh broccoli instead of frozen and one large chopped onion.

LOADED POTATO SOUP

Prep time: 25 minutes | *Makes about 6 1 1/2-cup servings*

This restaurant favorite is super simple to make at home, thanks to frozen diced hash brown potatoes, packaged bacon pieces, and dried minced onion.

---

1 14-oz can chicken broth (or 2 C. water plus 2 chicken bouillon cubes)

1 32-oz. pkg. frozen diced hash brown potatoes

2 3-oz. pkg. real bacon pieces (about 1 1/2 C.)

1/4 C. dried chopped onion

1 1/2 C. milk

1 8-oz. pkg. cream cheese

1 1/2 C. shredded sharp cheddar, divided

Salt and pepper to taste

1. Place chicken broth in a 4-quart stockpot over high heat. Add potatoes, all but 1/2 C. of the bacon pieces, onion flakes, and milk.

2. Cover with lid and bring soup to a gentle boil, about 7–10 minutes. Remove lid, turn heat to medium-low, stirring well so that potatoes cook evenly. Cook another 5 minutes, or until potatoes are tender.

3. While soup is cooking, cut cream cheese into large chunks and shred cheese if needed.

4. When potatoes are tender, stir in cream cheese and 1 C. of cheddar cheese, and mix until cheeses are melted and well blended with soup.

5. Allow soup to sit off heat an additional 5 minutes to thicken. Serve each bowl garnished with a spoonful each of the remaining bacon and cheddar.

Microwave directions:

1. Place broth, potatoes, bacon pieces, dried onion, and milk in a large microwavable bowl. Microwave, covered, on high for 12–15 minutes, stirring halfway through cooking time to distribute heat evenly.

2. While soup cooks, cut cream cheese into slices or chunks.

3. Stir in cream cheese and mix until well blended. Microwave, covered, an additional 5 minutes, or until potatoes are tender. While soup is cooking, shred cheese.

Stir in 1 C. of cheese. If soup becomes too thick, thin with a little chicken stock or milk. Serve garnished with a heaping spoonful each of the reserved bacon and cheddar.

Slow cooker directions: Place all ingredients except cheddar and reserved bacon in a slow cooker. Stir to mix then cook, covered, on high for about 3 hours, on low for about 5–6 hours, stirring once or twice during the cooking period so the soup cooks evenly. Stir in 1 C. shredded cheese 5 minutes before serving. Top each bowl with reserved 1/2 C. cheddar and reserved 1/2 C. bacon.

CREAMY TOMATO TORTELLINI SOUP

Prep time: 30 minutes | Makes 6 1 1/2-cup servings

Many tortellini soup recipes call for cooking the pasta in a separate pot. This recipe eliminates that step by cooking the tortellini in broth, then adding the rest of the soup ingredients. The cream cheese thickens the soup and adds richness. You can use light cream cheese, but plan on whisking it longer to remove any lumps.

2 14-oz. cans (or 4 C.) vegetable or chicken broth
1 9-oz. pkg. refrigerated cheese tortellini
1 6-oz. can tomato paste
1 15-oz. can diced tomatoes
1 tsp. dried basil
1 Tbsp. dried chopped onion
1/3 C. frozen chopped green pepper (or about 1/4 C. fresh)
1 Tbsp. sugar
1 tsp. garlic powder
1 C. milk
8 oz. cream cheese
Salt and pepper to taste
1/2 C. shredded cheddar or Parmesan, optional

1. In a large pot, bring broth to a boil. Add tortellini to broth and cook 5 minutes.

2. Stir in tomato paste and tomatoes, basil, onion, peppers, sugar, garlic, and milk. Turn heat to medium and allow mixture to simmer about 10 minutes.

3. While soup simmers, cut cream cheese in several chunks. Add chunks to soup and whisk until thoroughly incorporated.

4. Let soup simmer about 5 minutes more to allow flavors to blend. Add salt and pepper to taste. Serve topped with chopped green peppers, herbs, cheddar or Parmesan cheese.

Option: Add 1 to 2 C. chopped, cooked chicken during the last 10 minutes of cooking time.

MINESTRONE

Prep time: 30 minutes (20 minutes if using frozen vegetables.) | *Makes 6 1 1/2-cup servings*

Packaged bacon pieces, V-8 juice, and pesto take the shortcut route to robust flavor. Even after slicing the celery, carrots, and zucchini, the soup is ready to serve in thirty minutes. The secret is to thinly slice the celery and carrots and get them cooking right away. The other veggies cook more quickly. If you prefer to use frozen veggies, you may find a blend in your frozen foods aisle that incorporates the carrots, green beans, zucchini, and celery all in one package.

1 Tbsp. canola oil

1 C. frozen onion, slightly thawed

1 C. sliced celery, about 2 medium stalks

1 C. sliced carrots, about 1/3 of a 1-lb. bag of peeled baby carrots

1 3-oz. pkg. real bacon pieces, or more, to taste

2 12-oz. cans V-8 juice

4 C. water

1 C. frozen green beans

1 1/2 C. rotini, penne or bowtie pasta

1 C. sliced zucchini, about 1 small zucchini

1 15-oz. can cannellini or any small white beans, drained and rinsed

1 7-oz. container (about 1 C.) fresh pesto (Buittoni)

1. Heat oil over low heat in a large stockpot.

2. Meanwhile, thinly slice celery and carrots. Turn up heat and add celery, carrots and onion to pot. Cook for about 5 minutes, stirring occasionally.

3. Add bacon, V-8 juice, water, green beans, and pasta. Allow soup to come to a gentle boil.

4. Meanwhile, slice zucchini. After soup has gently boiled about 5 minutes, add zucchini, white beans, and pesto to pot. Stir to mix well. Allow the soup to cook another 5–10 minutes, or until pasta and vegetables are tender.

MINTED PEA SOUP

Prep time: 20 minutes | Makes about 6 1-cup servings

Traditional "spring pea soups" use fresh peas straight from the garden. But if you use frozen peas, you don't have to worry about shelling them, and you can make it any time of year. I tried this soup two ways: one with a cup of cream stirred in; the other a container of Greek yogurt. The cream gave it a velvety smoothness. The yogurt gave it a little tang. So the choice is up to you. Avoid overcooking the peas; you'll want to keep their bright color and flavor. You can serve this soup chilled if desired.

1. Place peas, broth, onion, and garlic powder in 2- or 3-quart microwavable bowl. Cover and microwave on high for 8–10 minutes, until peas are hot throughout.

2. Remove from heat; add mint.

3. Puree in two batches in a stand blender, or use a hand-held blender. Stir in yogurt or cream. Serve warm or chilled.

4 C. frozen peas, partially thawed
1 14-oz. can chicken broth, or 2 chicken bouillon cubes and 2 C. water
2 Tbsp. dried chopped onion
1 tsp. garlic powder
2 Tbsp. fresh mint or 2 tsp. dried mint (more if desired)
1 6-oz. carton Greek or plain yogurt, or 1 C. of cream
Salt and pepper to taste

BIGGEST LOSER RESORT'S ROASTED RED PEPPER BISQUE

Prep time: 45 minutes | Makes about 6 1-cup servings

In 2010 I visited the Biggest Loser Resort at Fitness Ridge in Southern Utah, where fans of the TV reality show embrace the workouts and spa cuisine. The resort shared this recipe with me. It didn't include directions for roasting and peeling the peppers, so I've added a hassle-free method. Roasting gives the peppers a deeper, sweeter flavor. The original recipe calls for fresh onion and herbs; I've included time-saving dried versions. I've also decreased the original amount of basil and thyme because tasters found them overpowering. Taste the finished soup and add more if you want. It's easier to add more than to subtract it. Agave is a natural sweetener that comes from a cactuslike plant. It's popular with low-carb dieters because it doesn't raise blood sugar levels. If you don't have agave, add about one and a half tablespoons of sugar to taste. This will change the calorie and nutrition content, of course.

4–5 large red bell peppers
1 C. sliced yellow onion (or about 1 1/2 C. frozen chopped)
2 Tbsp. chopped garlic (or 2 tsp. garlic powder)
3 C. vegetable or chicken stock (or use 2 14-oz. cans)
3 Tbsp. chopped fresh basil (1 Tbsp. dried basil; add more if desired)
1/2 Tbsp. fresh thyme (1/2 tsp. dried thyme; add more to taste if desired)
2 Tbsp. agave syrup (or 1 1/2 Tbsp. sugar to taste)
1 tsp. sea salt
1/2 tsp. black pepper

1. To roast the peppers, cut top and bottom half-inch from each pepper so that it's an open cylinder. With your fingers, clean out seeds. Then make a vertical slit down each pepper so that it can be flattened.

2. Place each flat pepper skin-side up on a baking sheet. Place tops and bottoms of peppers on baking sheet as well. Place in oven on top rack, and turn oven to broil on high heat. Broil for 5–10 minutes, until skin blisters and forms a few charred spots.

3. Turn off broiler and let peppers sit in the oven an additional 5 minutes. Then, with tongs, place in zip-locking freezer bag or plastic container with tight-fitting lid. Seal bag or lid and wait 15 minutes for steam to engage peel. Grasp peel next to blistered spots and pull off.

4. While waiting for peppers to cool, slice onion and chop garlic, if using fresh versions.

5. In nonstick pot, sauté onion and garlic over medium-high heat until soft, about 2 minutes. (Do not use oil; nonstick surface should keep from sticking.)

6. Add vegetable stock and roasted peppers. Bring to a boil, then reduce heat and simmer 10 minutes, until vegetables are tender.

7. Fill a stand blender half full of soup. Add herbs and agave; blend until smooth. Repeat with remaining soup until all of the soup is blended.

8. Pour soup back into pot. Taste and add salt, pepper, and any additional herbs, if desired. Reheat soup and serve hot.

Nutrients per serving: Approximately 59 calories, 1 gram fat, 3 grams protein, 12 grams carbohydrates, 1 gram dietary fiber.

— The Biggest Loser Resort

MAPLE-KISSED BUTTERNUT SQUASH BISQUE

Prep time: 40 minutes | Makes 6 1 1/2-cup servings

Many butternut squash soups call for peeling the squash before cooking, which can be awkward and time-consuming. Instead, cut the squash in pieces, microwave until tender, then scoop the pulp from the skin to puree in a blender. You'll want to let the squash cool five to ten minutes before handling. Or, check out your grocery store; some supermarkets carry frozen cooked squash, or fresh peeled and diced butternut squash. These options can cut your prep time in half. You can use fat-free half-and-half or milk with this recipe. For a richer texture, use cream. For a vegan dish, use vegetable stock and soy milk.

1 large butternut squash
1 C. apple juice or cider
1 tsp. salt
1 tsp. thyme
2 Tbsp. maple-flavored syrup (or more to taste)
1/4 tsp. ground nutmeg, optional
1 pint (2 C.) fat-free half-and-half, regular half-and-half, or soy milk
1 tsp. garlic powder
1 can chicken or vegetable broth
Several grinds of pepper

1. Cut squash in half and scoop out seeds and pulp.

2. Cut each half into thirds or quarters and place in large microwavable bowl with lid. Add about 1/2 C. water to bowl.

3. Microwave, covered, on high for 15–20 minutes, or until flesh is tender when fork is inserted.

4. Remove from microwave, take off cover, and scoop the squash onto a plate or tray. Allow to the squash to cool for 5–10 minutes.

5. Using a large spoon, scoop the flesh from the skins of about half of the squash pieces, and place in a blender. Add apple juice, salt, thyme, syrup, and nutmeg. Place lid on with middle hole removed and puree until smooth. Pour puree back into large bowl.

6. Scoop flesh from the remaining squash pieces and add to blender with half-and-half. Puree until smooth and add to large bowl with garlic and vegetable broth. Stir to mix well. Taste, and add more salt, pepper, or maple syrup if desired.

7. Microwave on high 2–3 minutes to heat soup through. Serve with a swirl of cream or half-and-half.

CREAMY CAULIFLOWER SOUP

Prep time: 30 minutes | Makes 6 1 1/2-cup servings

Although it's not as popular as its emerald cousin, broccoli, cauliflower is a healthy veggie. It contains high amounts of vitamins C and K, among other nutrients. The pureed cauliflower provides part of the creamy texture of this soup; the cheeses provide richness. Frozen chopped cauliflower makes for no-hassle preparation.

3 12-oz. pkg. frozen cauliflower pieces
1 can chicken or vegetable broth
2 Tbsp. dried chopped onion
 1 1/2 C. milk (or fat-free half-and-half)
1 8-oz. pkg. cream cheese (or light cream cheese)
1 C. grated sharp cheddar cheese
Freshly ground pepper to taste
Salt to taste
Cheddar cheese for garnish, optional

1. Place cauliflower pieces in a 4-quart stockpot with broth and dried onion. Cover and bring broth to a gentle boil. Reduce heat to medium, and cook cauliflower for about 10 minutes, until tender.

2. Using a ladle, transfer cauliflower to a blender.

3. Turn blender on low and puree for one or two minutes before turning to high (to avoid steam building up or liquid sloshing). Add 1/2 C. of the milk if mixture becomes too thick. Puree until smooth. Or use an immersion blender to puree.

4. Return soup to pot, on low heat, and stir in remaining milk, cream cheese, and cheddar, whisking until well blended. Thin with additional milk or chicken broth if necessary.

5. Add salt and pepper to taste. Serve topped with more cheese if desired.

CHEESY VEGGIE CHOWDER

Prep time: 30 minutes | *Makes about 6 1 1/2-cup servings*

No peeling or chopping required for this fast chowder! Feel free to experiment with adding other favorite vegetables. Add the peas near the end of cooking time so they keep their bright color.

2 14-oz. cans chicken broth (or 4 bouillon cubes plus 3 3/4 C. water)
1 28-oz. pkg. frozen Southern-style hash browns O'Brien
2 Tbsp. dried chopped onion
1 1/2 C. frozen diced carrots (or about 1 C. fresh sliced carrots)
1 lb. Velveeta processed cheese
1 C. milk
1 12-oz. pkg. frozen chopped broccoli
1 C. frozen peas
Salt and pepper to taste

1. Pour broth in a large (4-quart) pot over high heat. Add hash browns, onion, and carrots; cover and allow broth to come to a gentle boil.

2. Cook 10 minutes, or until potatoes and carrots are almost tender.

3. While vegetables are cooking, cut Velveeta cheese into large slices or chunks.

4. Lower heat to medium and stir in Velveeta, milk, and broccoli. Simmer another 10 minutes, stirring occasionally, until broccoli is tender and Velveeta is melted.

5. Stir in peas. Taste and add salt or pepper as desired. Allow soup to stand, off heat, for about 5 minutes before serving. Garnish with shredded cheese, bacon, or parsley.

Options: If you have time, you can add chopped vegetables such as celery or cauliflower during the cooking process.

QUICK VEGETARIAN VEGGIE SOUP

Prep time: 30 minutes | *Makes about 6 1 1/4-cup servings*

In this soup, V-8 juice offers a variety of vegetable flavors, including a strong tomato presence. If it's fresh tomato season, feel free to substitute about six medium tomatoes, peeled and pureed, for the V-8 juice. Otherwise, there's no peeling or chopping required.

1 Tbsp. olive oil
1 1/2 C. frozen chopped onion
4 to 5 C. frozen vegetable blend of
   green beans, corn, peas, and
   carrots
2 14-oz. cans vegetable broth
1 12-oz. can V-8 juice
1 Tbsp. garlic powder
1/2 tsp. dried thyme
1/2 tsp. dried basil
1/2 tsp. sugar
Freshly ground pepper to taste
Salt to taste

1. Heat olive oil over medium-high heat. Add onion and sauté, stirring, for about 5 minutes, until limp.

2. Add frozen vegetables, broth, V-8 juice, seasonings, and sugar.

3. Simmer 10–15 minutes, or until vegetables are tender.

4. Taste and add salt and pepper if needed.

Options: Mix it up by adding other less-familiar root veggies such as parsnips, turnips, or rutabagas.

CURRIED CARROT BISQUE

Prep time: 30 minutes | *Makes about 6 1-1/4-cup servings*

Sautéing the carrots brings out some of the vegetable's natural sweetness. The dairy mellows the strong carrot flavor. To save fat and calories, you can use fat-free half-and-half or milk instead of cream.

1. Melt butter in a 4-quart stockpot. Add carrots and onion, sauté over medium-high heat for 5–10 minutes, stirring, until onion is translucent and carrots begin to brown on edges. Don't let them burn.

2. Add chicken stock, salt, sugar, garlic, and curry powder.

3. Cover pot. Bring to a gentle boil for 12–15 minutes, until carrots are tender.

4. Remove pot from the heat and stir in cream.

5. Puree soup with an immersion blender or in two batches in stand blender. Don't fill blender more than half full, and start on lowest setting and then move to high, to avoid splashing.

Garnish with another swirl of cream and/or a sprinkle of nuts.

2–3 Tbsp. butter
2 lbs. baby carrots
1 C. frozen chopped onion
2 cans chicken stock
1–2 tsp. salt to taste
2 tsp. brown sugar
1 tsp. garlic powder
2 tsp. mild curry powder
1 C. cream or half-and-half

CREAM OF ASPARAGUS SOUP

Prep time: 30 minutes | Makes about 6 1-cup servings

Crisp-tender asparagus pieces are suspended in a creamy broth. Let the asparagus cook for only a few minutes so it doesn't become overcooked and mushy.

1 Tbsp. butter
1 lb. fresh asparagus
2 14-oz. cans chicken or vegetable broth
1 1/2 C. frozen chopped onion
Pinch of crushed red pepper flakes
3 Tbsp. cornstarch
1/3 C. water
1 C. cream or half-and-half (fat-free half-and-half is okay)
Salt and pepper to taste

1. Melt butter in a 4-quart stockpot over low heat while you wash and cut asparagus. Trim off woody bottom inch of stalks and discard. Cut rest of stalks into 1-inch pieces.

2. Turn stockpot heat to medium-high and add onion. Cook 4 to 5 minutes, until soft.

3. Add broth, asparagus, and red pepper flakes to pot and bring to a gentle boil. Let asparagus cook 1 to 2 minutes.

4. With tongs, remove about a dozen asparagus tips from pot and reserve in ice water to preserve bright green color.

5. Mix cornstarch with water until smooth and stir into gently boiling broth. Keep stirring as broth thickens, about 3–5 minutes. Asparagus should be crisp-tender but not mushy.

6. Turn off heat. Add cream and stir to a smooth consistency.

7. Taste and add salt and pepper as needed.

8. Ladle into small bowls or cups and garnish each bowl with two of the reserved asparagus tips.

Options: Serve with oyster crackers or chopped nuts for added crunch.

FENNEL BISQUE

Prep time: 30 minutes | Makes about 6 1-cup servings

Never thought about fennel as a soup? Neither did I until I tried a bowl at McCrady's in Charleston, South Carolina. This historic tavern-turned-restaurant was opened in 1788, and George Washington visited there in 1791. After I came home from Charleston, I came up with a recipe that captures the fennel's licorice-like flavor, but is simple to prepare.

3 bulbs fennel, with stalks and
    feathery green tops (about 2–3
    lbs.)
2 Tbsp. butter
About 1 1/2 C. chopped frozen onion
    (about 1 C. fresh)
1 tsp. garlic powder
2 cans (about 4 C.) chicken stock
1 C. half-and-half
Salt and freshly ground black pepper

1. Heat butter in a 3- or 4-quart soup pot over low heat.

2. Remove green fronds from fennel stalks and reserve. Coarsely slice fennel bulbs and stalks.

3. Turn heat to medium-high. When butter begins sizzling, add onion and fennel and cook, stirring, about 5 minutes, until they become slightly softened. Stir to keep from burning.

4. Add garlic powder and chicken stock and increase heat to high. Bring soup to a gentle boil and cook until fennel is tender, about 10 minutes.

5. Puree soup, in batches, in a blender until smooth. If you prefer a super-smooth soup, strain through a strainer into a serving pot or bowl.

6. Add half-and-half and season with salt and pepper.

7. Serve garnished with fennel fronds and dots of olive oil.

FRENCH ONION SOUP WITH PARMESAN CROUTONS

Prep time: 30 minutes | *Makes about 6 1 1/2-cup servings*

Since onions are the star of this soup, you need to slice up fresh ones—you can't get away with using frozen or dried. While you're at it, you might as well mince fresh garlic too. There's something heavenly about the aroma of the caramelizing onion and garlic! Even with the peeling, slicing, and caramelizing onion, this soup still can be on the table in less than thirty minutes. Many recipes say to ladle out the soup, then top it with a baguette slice, then top that with cheese and place all the bowls of soup under a broiler until the cheese bubbles. Toasting cheese-topped croutons first then placing it on the soup cuts the risk of sloshing hot soup while getting it in and out of the oven.

1/4 C. butter or olive oil
4 large onions, thinly sliced
3 cloves of garlic, minced
1 tsp. brown sugar
1/2 tsp. dried rosemary
1 tsp. dried thyme
3 cans beef broth
Freshly ground pepper to taste
1 1/2 C. croutons
1/2 C. shredded Parmesan cheese

1. Heat butter and olive oil in a 4- to 6-quart stockpot over low heat, while peeling and thinly slicing onions. (Cut each onion in half and set flat side on cutting board. Then slice into 1/8- to 1/4-inch slices. Mince the garlic.

2. When onions are sliced, turn heat to high. Add onions to sizzling oil or butter and stir continually for about 5 minutes, until they begin to turn golden. Take care not to let them to burn.

3. Turn heat to medium and add brown sugar, garlic, rosemary, and thyme, and continue stirring onions for about 10–15 more minutes. Onions should be deep golden and sticky.

4. Add broth; bring soup to a gentle boil for 5 more minutes. Add several grinds of pepper to taste.

5. While soup is cooking, preheat broiler and spread croutons evenly on a pie tin. Sprinkle Parmesan over them.

6. Place in oven on broil for 3–4 minutes, until cheese is bubbly with golden-brown edges (don't wait too long or croutons will burn!). Ladle soup in six bowls and top each serving with about 1/4 C. of croutons.

ZUCCHINI AND BACON SOUP

Prep time: 30 minutes | Makes about 6 1 1/2-cup servings

This is a great way to use the zucchini your neighbors keep leaving on your doorstep at harvest time! Try to use small or medium-sized zucchini for this soup; the large ones are tough and seedy.

2 14-oz. cans chicken broth

3 lbs. zucchini (8–9 C. of chunks, about 5 medium zucchini)

1 C. chopped frozen onion (or about 3 Tbsp. dried onion flakes)

1 3-oz. pkg. real bacon bits (about 3/4 C.)

2 C. half-and-half, or fat-free half-and-half

1 tsp. freshly ground pepper

1. Heat broth over low while slicing zucchini in chunks about 1-inch thick.

2. Turn heat to high and place zucchini, onion, and bacon in pot.

3. When liquid comes to a boil, turn heat to medium and cover with lid, allowing mixture to simmer 10–12 minutes. (Or place in a large microwavable casserole dish, cover, and microwave for 10–12 minutes).

4. Remove pot from heat and allow mixture cool several minutes.

5. Puree with a hand-held blender or in two batches in a stand blender. Start with blender on lowest speed then move to high to reduce splashing.

6. Return to pan. Add cream or milk and pepper to taste. Reheat and serve.

GAZPACHO

Prep time: 20 minutes | Makes about 6 1-cup servings

Gazpacho, the Spanish cold soup, was trendy in the 1960s when Americans went through their "international cuisine" phase, embracing British fish 'n' chips and Swiss fondue as well. It's still a popular soup to slurp during hot summer days, and full of nutrition as well. If it's fresh tomato season, substitute them for some of the V-8 juice.

1. Cut bell pepper, cucumber, and celery in chunks.

2. Place in blender with 1 can V-8 juice, onion, and garlic. Puree until chunky-smooth.

3. Pour into large serving bowl or tureen. Add remaining V-8 juice and balsamic vinegar.

4. Cover and refrigerate until well chilled. Season to taste with hot sauce, salt, and pepper. Serve garnished with chopped cucumber, avocado, jicama, or croutons.

Option: For a creamy soup, add 1 slice of bread, crust removed, to the blender with soup.

1 large red or green bell pepper, cut in chunks
1 small cucumber, cut in chunks
1 celery stalk, cut in chunks
3 12-oz. cans V-8 juice (substitute about 6 medium peeled and pureed tomatoes per 1 can of V-8)
2 Tbsp. dried chopped onion
1 tsp. garlic powder
Drops of hot sauce to taste
2 tsp. balsamic vinegar
Salt and pepper to taste
Garnish: Chopped cucumber, jicama, avocado, or croutons.

GARDEN TOMATO BISQUE

Prep time: 35 minutes if using fresh tomatoes, 20 minutes if using canned tomatoes | Makes about 6 1 1/2-cup servings

This is a great way to use fresh in-season tomatoes from your garden, if you have them. If not, use canned, diced tomatoes. By immersing the fresh tomatoes in boiling water for about thirty seconds, and then in ice water, their peels slip off easily.

10–12 large peeled and chopped tomatoes (or 3 14.5-oz. cans diced tomatoes)
2 Tbsp. olive oil
1 C. frozen diced onion
1 6-oz. can tomato paste
2 tsp. dried basil (2 Tbsp. fresh, chopped)
1/2 tsp. dried thyme
1 tsp. dried oregano
2 tsp. garlic powder or minced garlic
2 Tbsp. sugar, or to taste
2 C. chicken broth (or 2 C. water plus 2 chicken bouillon cubes)
1 C. cream or half-and-half (fat-free is okay)
Salt and pepper to taste

1. Peel and chop tomatoes: Fill a pot halfway with water, cover, and place on stove over high heat until water boils rapidly, 3–5 minutes. While waiting, cut a shallow X in the bottom of each tomato. With tongs, immerse several tomatoes in water (as many as can be completely immersed). Wait about 30 seconds. While waiting, fill another bowl or pot halfway full with cold water and ice cubes. Use tongs to remove tomatoes and set them in ice water for one or two minutes, while you add more tomatoes to boiling water. When all tomatoes have sat in ice bath, tug on their skins at the X, and slip off skins. Remove each core and rough-chop the tomatoes on a cutting board.

2. While peeling tomatoes, heat oil over low heat in a 4-quart stockpot. When you are ready to cook the onion, turn heat to high. Cook and stir onion over high until softened, about 5 minutes.

3. Add all ingredients except milk or cream, and bring to a gentle boil. Cook 10 minutes. Stir in cream or milk and remove from heat.

4. Serve soup chunky-style, or allow the soup to cool a few minutes and then puree in two batches in a stand blender, or use an immersion blender. Taste and add salt if needed. Garnish with chopped basil or a basil sprig.

HARVEST PUMPKIN SOUP WITH CHEDDAR

Prep time: 30 minutes | *Makes about 6 1 1/2-cup servings*

I've been flattered at the many requests and compliments I've received since I created this recipe in 2001. It gives credence to the theory that if you add enough bacon, cream, or cheese, you can make anything taste great! Ironically, no one else in my own family will give this soup a try ("Pumpkin? Ew!"). So, sometimes I'll make a half batch for myself and have one bowl each day until it's gone. Sometimes I don't add the cheese, since the soup is pretty rich all by itself.

2 tsp. canola oil
1 C. frozen chopped onion
5 C. chicken broth (or 3 14-oz. cans chicken broth)
1 29-oz. can solid-pack pumpkin (NOT pumpkin pie mix)
1 2.5-oz. pkg. cooked bacon pieces (about 1/2 C.)
1 Tbsp. sugar
1/2 tsp. dried thyme
1 C. cream or half-and-half (or fat-free half-and-half)
1/4 tsp. ground nutmeg
1 tsp. curry powder (optional)
1 C. grated sharp cheddar cheese
Pumpkin seeds for garnish (optional)

1. Add oil to pot and turn heat to high.

2. Add onion and sauté, stirring, until it begins to soften and turn golden, about 10 minutes.

3. Stir in stock, pumpkin, bacon, sugar, and thyme. Bring to a gentle boil. Reduce heat to medium-high, and simmer about 5 minutes.

4. Remove soup from heat and add cream, nutmeg, and curry powder, if desired.

5. Puree soup in two or three batches in blender, leaving middle of lid open to avoid pressure buildup of steam. Start on low speed to prevent splashing. Or use an immersion blender.

6. Season with salt and pepper. When serving, spoon a little cheese on top of each bowl of soup. Garnish with pumpkin seeds if desired.

Option: Substitute Parmesan cheese for the cheddar topping.

MEGA-MUSHROOM SOUP

Prep time: 30 minutes | *Makes about 6 1 1/4-cup servings*

This soup's deep, earthy flavor comes from dried, fresh, and canned mushrooms. You can puree it for a smooth texture or leave some of the mushrooms chunky.

1 1-oz. pkg. dried mixed wild mushrooms
2 cans beef broth (or vegetable broth)
2 Tbsp. butter or olive oil
2 8-oz. pkg. fresh, sliced cremini or button mushrooms
1 medium onion, sliced or chopped (or about 1 1/2 C. frozen chopped onion)
1 tsp. dried rosemary
1/2 tsp. dried thyme
1 small can sliced mushrooms, stems and pieces
1 1/2 C. cream or half-and-half

1. Place dried mushrooms in a microwavable 3-C. bowl. Pour 1 can of broth over mushrooms.

2. Cover and microwave for 3 minutes, or until stock is boiling. Remove from microwave and allow mushrooms to steep in broth for about 10 minutes.

3. While mushrooms are steeping, melt butter in a 2-quart saucepan on low heat while you slice or chop onion.

4. Turn heat to medium-high and add fresh mushrooms and onion. Cook about 10 minutes, stirring so that vegetables don't burn.

5. Pour reconstituted mushroom/broth mixture, rosemary, thyme, cooked mushroom/onion mixture, and canned mushrooms in blender, making sure to scrape pan for any browned bits. Puree until smooth.

6. Pour back into saucepan and stir in remaining can of beef broth and cream. Allow to cook until heated through.

Options: For a chunky texture, only puree the reconstituted mushrooms and half of the mushroom/onion mixture. Also, if fresh wild mushrooms are available, they make a nice addition.

ROASTED GARLIC BISQUE

Prep time: 1 hour, 15 minutes, Active prep time: 30 minutes | *Makes about 6 1 1/2-cup servings*

I fell in love with a roasted garlic soup at Emeril Lagasse's NOLA restaurant in New Orleans. But the recipes I found for similar soups take several hours to make, so I shortened and simplified. One step I couldn't skip was roasting the garlic; it mellows the harshness and results in a sweet, nutty flavor. It involves some wait time, but my method takes little effort. Instead of peeling each individual clove of garlic, roast the five heads of garlic, unpeeled, in a small casserole dish covered with a lid. After they cool, squeeze out as much pulp as possible. Then steep the peels to help flavor the broth.

5 large heads of garlic
4 14-oz. cans chicken broth
2 Tbsp. butter
2 C. frozen chopped onion (or about
    1 1/2 C. fresh)
1 Tbsp. ready minced fresh garlic or 1
    1/2 tsp. garlic powder
3 C. purchased garlic-flavored
    croutons
1/2 tsp. freshly ground pepper
1 C. cream (or fat-free half-and-half)
3/4 C. grated Parmesan cheese
Salt to taste
Additional croutons or chopped
    parsley or basil for garnish

1. Peel away outer layers of skin on garlic bulbs, leaving skins of individual cloves intact. Using a knife, cut off about 1/4 inch from top of cloves, exposing the individual cloves of garlic. Place garlic in a glass casserole dish with a lid; or wrap in foil. Place in oven at 375 degrees for 30–35 minutes, or until garlic is very soft. Allow garlic to cool about 15 minutes before handling.

2. Squeeze roasted garlic pulp from peels into a small bowl and set aside. Reserve empty garlic peels.

3. Place 2 cans chicken broth and reserved empty garlic heads back in glass casserole dish and microwave on high for 5 minutes. Turn setting to low and simmer an additional 5 minutes, and allow the liquid to steep 5 more minutes.

4. While garlic heads are steeping, heat butter in a 4-quart large stockpot over medium-high heat. Cook onion, stirring, until slightly caramelized, 5 to 7 minutes. Stir in roasted garlic and minced garlic, or garlic powder.

5. Use a strainer to strain steeped garlic/stock mixture into stockpot, pushing on garlic peels to get out all flavorful juices. Discard peels.

6. Add remaining 2 cans of chicken broth to pot, along with croutons and pepper. Bring the mixture to a low boil while stirring so that croutons dissolve into soup, about 5 minutes.

7. Remove soup from heat. With an immersion blender, or in batches in blender, puree soup until smooth.

8. Pour soup back into pot over low heat and add cream and cheese; stir until well blended.

9. Garnish each serving with additional croutons, or chopped parsley or basil. Thin soup with a little chicken stock or milk if needed.

GARDEN VEGETABLE SOUP

Prep time: 30 minutes | *Makes about 6 1 1/4-cup servings*

Since these veggies play starring roles in this soup, it's best to use fresh. Sautéing the onions, carrot, mushrooms, and celery until they are golden will coax a little more flavor from them. Tomato paste and mushrooms give a flavor boost without meat so that your soup will taste like real soup instead of waterlogged veggies. I suggest you use a quality vegetable broth instead of a generic brand. I used Swanson, but I'm sure expensive organic broths are also good. Even with some slicing and chopping, the soup still comes together in less than 30 minutes. Using preshredded coleslaw mix shaves off time, and you might find fresh prechopped onions, carrots, and celery at your supermarket.

2 Tbsp. canola or olive oil
1 large onion, chopped (about 1 1/2 C.)
2 stalks celery (about 1 1/4 C.)
1 1/2 C. sliced carrots (about half of a
    1-lb. bag of baby carrots)
1 1/2 C. sliced, chopped mushrooms
2 C. shredded cabbage (bagged
    coleslaw mix)
3 cloves garlic, minced (or 1 1/2 tsp.
    garlic powder)
3 14-oz. cans vegetable broth
1/2 tsp. dried thyme
1/2 tsp. dried basil
2 Tbsp. tomato paste
1 bay leaf
1 C. sliced zucchini, optional
1 C. fresh or frozen green beans,
    optional
Salt to taste
Freshly ground pepper to taste

1. Heat oil in a 4-to-6-quart stockpot over low heat while you chop onion and slice celery and carrots.

2. Turn heat to medium-high and cook onion, celery, carrots, and mushrooms for about 10 minutes, stirring almost constantly. Onion should be golden and caramelized.

3. Add cabbage, garlic, broth, thyme, basil, tomato paste, bay leaf, and zucchini, or fresh green beans, if desired. Bring soup to a gentle boil and cook for 10 more minutes. Add freshly ground salt and pepper to taste.

EASY CHEESY
POTATO-BROCCOLI SOUP

Prep time: 25 minutes | Makes 6 1 1/2–cup servings

This soup has virtually no prep work, thanks to two boxes of julienne-style au gratin potato mix and frozen chopped broccoli. If you can't find a boxed mix with julienne-cut potatoes, you can use a sliced variety. If you use broccoli cuts instead of chopped broccoli, add another 5 minutes to the cooking time.

1. Pour the dried potatoes from their packets in a large 4-quart microwavable bowl.

2. Add with the chicken broth and water. Cover and microwave for 10 minutes on high.

3. Stir in the seasoning packets from the potato mix, as well as the broccoli, milk, and bacon bits, until well mixed.

4. Cover and cook an additional 10 minutes on high, or until potatoes and broccoli are tender.

5. Stir in cheddar cheese. Let soup sit a few minutes before serving.

2 4.5-oz. pkg. au gratin julienned potatoes (such as Betty Crocker)
2 14-oz. cans chicken broth
1 14-oz. can water (use the chicken broth can)
1 12-oz. pkg. frozen chopped broccoli
1 Tbsp. dried minced onion flakes
1/4 C. bacon bits, optional
2 C. milk
1/2 C. shredded sharp cheddar cheese

SILKEN POTATO LEEK SOUP

Prep time: 25 minutes | *Makes 6 1 1/4-cup servings*

This classic soup has a silky texture and delicate flavor. A package of Southern-style hash brown potatoes makes this a snap. You can peel and dice fresh ones, but you'll need more cooking time. Unfortunately. there's no getting away from chopping leeks. These are like giant green onions or scallions. Cook the white and barely green part with the potatoes and use snips of the dark green part as a garnish.

2 Tbsp. butter

4 large leeks

2 tsp. garlic powder or 2 cloves garlic, or 2 tsp. minced garlic

2 14-oz. cans chicken broth (or 4 C. water plus 4 chicken bouillon cubes)

1 32-oz. bag frozen Southern-style hash brown potatoes

1 tsp. salt to taste

1/2 tsp. freshly ground pepper, or to taste

1 C. cream, milk or half-and-half

1. Melt butter over low heat in a 4- to-6-quart stockpot.

2. Meanwhile, rinse leeks, and on a cutting board using a chef's knife, slice off roots at the bottom of each leek. Slice white and barely green parts of each leek in about 1/4-inch slices. You should have about 1 1/2 to 2 C. white and light-green slices. Reserve some of dark-green parts.

3. Raise heat to high and add white and light-green leek slices and garlic. Stir to separate leeks into thin rings and cook for 3–4 minutes, until leeks are wilted and fragrant.

4. Add the chicken broth, potatoes, salt, and pepper. Cover pot and bring soup to a gentle boil for about 10–15 minutes, until potatoes are tender and starting to fall apart.

4. Remove from the heat and stir in cream or milk.

5. Puree mixture in two batches on low speed in a stand blender; or use a hand-held blender to puree until barely smooth. (Don't overpuree or potatoes may become gluey.)

6. Taste and adjust seasonings if necessary. If soup seems too thick, thin with a little water or milk.

To serve, top with green leek slices.

ROSEMARY POTATO AND CORN CHOWDER

Prep time: 30 minutes | *Makes 6 1 1/2-cup servings*

Thanks to O'Brien-style frozen hash browns, you can avoid peeling or dicing potatoes, onions, and peppers. Packaged bacon bits eliminate the messy job of bacon frying, and they contain 50 percent less fat than regular bacon. Using fat-free half-and-half further slashes the fat and calories without losing flavor. You could also use skim milk, but your soup will be less thick and creamy. The rosemary gives a subtle pine-ish flavor.

2 14-oz. cans chicken broth (or 4 chicken bouillon cubes and 1 3/4 C. water)

1 28-oz. pkg. O'Brien-style diced hash brown potatoes

1 3-oz. pkg. shelf-stable bacon bits (or about 3/4 C. of cooked, chopped bacon or 1 C. finely diced ham)

1 15-oz. can corn, drained

2 tsp. dried rosemary or 1 Tbsp. fresh rosemary

3 Tbsp. cornstarch

1/4 C. water

1 1/2 C. half-and-half, fat-free half-and-half, or milk

1 tsp. freshly ground pepper

Optional garnishes: grated cheddar cheese, bacon bits, rosemary sprigs

1. Place chicken broth, potatoes, and bacon in a large pot over high heat.

2. When mixture comes to a boil, reduce heat to keep soup gently boiling, about 10 minutes, or until potatoes are tender. Add corn and rosemary.

3. Mix cornstarch and water to a smooth paste. Stir cornstarch mixture into gently boiling soup and continue stirring until soup thickens.

4. Turn off heat and stir in milk or half-and-half and pepper, until mixture is well blended and soup rethickens.

5. Taste soup and adjust seasonings as desired. Ladle into serving bowls; garnish each with a tsp. of shredded cheddar, bacon pieces, or a rosemary sprig.

Slow cooker directions: Place all ingredients except cornstarch and 1/4 C. of water in a slow cooker on high for 3–4 hours; on low for 5–6 hours. Mix cornstarch and water into a smooth paste and stir into soup. Turn soup to high and leave lid off, stirring occasionally, for 20–30 minutes, until soup thickens.

RICH MUSHROOM AND BROWN RICE SOUP

Prep time: 30 minutes | Makes about 6 1 1/2-cup servings

This hearty soup uses a combination of fresh and dried mushrooms to create a deep, earthy flavor.
Quick-cooking brown rice adds a healthy, whole-grain touch without the long simmering time.

2 Tbsp. canola oil or butter
2 C. frozen onion, thawed if possible
16 to 20 oz. sliced cremini mushrooms
    (baby portobellos), about 5–6 C.
1/2 oz. pkg. dried porcini mushrooms,
    rinsed and finely chopped
3 14-oz. cans beef broth (or vegetable
    broth)
1 C. water
1 1/2 C. quick-cooking brown rice
    (such as Minute Rice)
2 tsp. garlic powder
1/2 tsp. dried sage
1/2 tsp. dried thyme
1 tsp. balsamic vinegar
1 tsp. dried chopped parsley (or 1
    Tbsp. fresh)
1 can condensed golden cream of
    mushroom soup
Several grinds of pepper

1. Heat oil or butter in a large 4-to 6-quart stockpot over high heat. Add onion and mushrooms and cook, stirring occasionally, about 10 minutes.

2. Turn heat to medium and continue to cook onion and mushrooms an additional 5 minutes, until mushrooms are brown.

3. Meanwhile rinse porcini mushrooms in a sieve. Using kitchen shears, snip porcinis into thin ribbons with kitchen shears. Add to pot.

4. Add beef broth, water, brown rice, garlic, sage, thyme, and balsamic vinegar. Turn heat to high and bring soup to a gentle boil. Cook 8 minutes, or until rice is almost tender.

5. While soup is cooking, place parsley in a 1/2 C. measuring cup. Snip with kitchen shears until chopped.

6. When rice is almost tender, stir in golden cream of mushroom soup, parsley, and pepper. Let the soup cook 1–2 more minutes, until rice is completely tender and flavors are blended.

HOTEL UTAH BORSCHT

Prep time: 30 minutes | *Makes 8 1-cup servings*

During my ten years as the Deseret News *food editor, the Hotel Utah's borscht was one of the most requested recipes. When it was built in downtown Salt Lake City in 1911, Hotel Utah was the premier hotel west of the Mississippi. Every US president from William Howard Taft to Ronald Reagan has stayed there. The hotel was closed in 1987, and some floors were renovated into office space for its owner, the Church of Jesus Christ of Latter-day Saints. The building still houses three restaurants, but none of them serves the borscht that was once so popular. Obviously, tastes have changed. But during the building's hundredth anniversary gala, it was one of the historic "signature" dishes served. Chef Don Sanchez of Temple Square Hospitality shared the recipe with me, noting that he made some changes to legendary Chef Girard's original version. "We used chicken stock instead of the beef stock, and we pureed the beets instead of just using the juice from the cooking process. Instead of adding the sour cream we used it as part of the garnish because I didn't like the color when we added the sour cream."*
For the sake of nostalgia, here's the original recipe. But if you have no qualms about tampering with history, feel free to switch it up as Sanchez did.

---

4 C. beet juice (or 4 C. pureed cooked beets)
4 C. chicken or beef broth, divided
Juice of 1 lemon
Sugar to taste

Salt to taste
1/4 C. cornstarch
1 C. sour cream
1 or 2 egg yolks
Chopped parsley
Hard-cooked eggs, diced
Lemon wedges

Bring beet juice and 3 1/2 C. of broth to boil in a pot. Stir in lemon juice, sugar, and salt. Combine remaining 1/2 C. broth and cornstarch until smooth. Stir into soup. Cook and stir until thickened.

Combine sour cream and egg yolks. Gradually stir 1 C. of hot beet juice mixture into egg mixture. Then, stirring constantly, slowly add warmed eggs back into hot liquid. Heat without boiling. Strain. Serve hot or cold.

Garnish with sour cream, parsley, and eggs. Serve with lemon wedges.

Slow Cooker Split Pea and Ham Soup................................140

West African-Style Peanut Soup...141

Thai-Style Peanut and Noodle Soup 142

Red Beans and Rice Soup 144

Tuscan Bean and Kale Soup 145

Chickpea and Spinach Soup..146

Spicy Black Bean Soup..148

Crunchy Almond-Celery Soup 149

Herbed Bean and Bacon Soup 150

Spicy Lentil and Sausage Stew..152

Slow Cooker Vegetarian Lentil Stew 154

Black Bean and Ham Soup 155

Fifteen-Bean Soup 156

BEAN AND NUT SOUPS

SLOW COOKER SPLIT PEA AND HAM SOUP

Total prep time: 3–4 hours or 6–8 hours, Active time: 5 minutes | *Makes 6 1 1/2-cup servings*

This stick-to-your ribs meal takes just five minutes to throw together; then your slow cooker does the rest of the work. You can find packages of diced ham in most supermarket meat cases.

1 16-oz. pkg. dried split peas
3 C. water
2 cans chicken stock
2 C. diced ham
1 12-oz. pkg. frozen mirepoix blend
    (or 2/3 C. fresh chopped onion,
    1/3 C. sliced celery, and 1/3 C.
    chopped carrot)
2 Tbsp. dried minced onion
1 bay leaf
1/2 tsp. dried thyme
1 tsp. hickory-flavored salt or liquid
    smoke, optional
Optional garnishes: Chopped parsley,
    ham, or bacon bits

1. Place all ingredients in a regular-size slower cooker.

2. Cover with lid and cook on high setting 3–5 hours, low for 6–8 hours.

3. To serve, garnish with chopped parsley, chopped ham, or bacon bits.

WEST AFRICAN-STYLE PEANUT SOUP

Prep time: 30 minutes | *Makes 6 1 1/2-cup servings*

"Groundnut" is the common African term for peanuts, and this curried soup is a shorthand version of "groundnut stew." Tomatoes and peanut butter? Who knew?

1. Heat oil in a large stockpot over low heat while you chop onions (if using fresh) and red bell peppers.

2. Turn heat to high and cook onion and bell peppers about 5 minutes.

3. Stir in garlic powder, tomatoes, chicken or vegetable broth, ginger, curry powder, pepper, and cayenne.

4. Simmer about 10 minutes. Add peanut butter and simmer five more minutes to blend the flavors. Taste, and add more ginger, curry, or cayenne if desired.

Options: If you have more time, add a handful of dried brown lentils or quick-cooking brown rice when you add the tomatoes and broth. Simmer about 20–30 minutes, or until lentils or rice are tender. This will give more body to soup.

1 Tbsp. olive oil
12 oz. frozen chopped onion, or 1 1/2 C. chopped (about 2 medium onions)
2 large red bell peppers, chopped (about 2 C.)
1 tsp. garlic powder
2 14.5-oz. cans petite-diced tomatoes
2 14-oz. cans vegetable or chicken broth
1 tsp. ginger
2 tsp. curry powder
1/2 tsp. freshly ground pepper
1/2 tsp. cayenne powder
1 1/4 C. peanut butter (crunchy or creamy)

THAI-STYLE PEANUT AND NOODLE SOUP

Prep time: 30 minutes | *Makes about 6 1 1/2-cup servings*

Instead of cooking the noodles separately, they are boiled in the chicken broth with the soup—no need to wash a second pan. You can use precooked chicken to save time making this creamy, nutty soup, or you can leave out the chicken for a meatless dish. If you use regular soy sauce, reduce the amount so that the soup isn't overly salty.

1 Tbsp. canola or peanut oil

1 large chicken breast, diced into 1/2 inch pieces or 1 C. cooked, diced chicken

4 14-oz. cans chicken broth

1 Tbsp. garlic powder

1 C. pineapple juice

1/2 C. reduced-sodium soy sauce (or 1/4 C. regular soy sauce)

4 oz. whole wheat or regular spaghetti or linguini noodles (1/4 of a 1-lb. pkg.)

2 tsp. red pepper flakes, or to taste

1 large red bell pepper, diced or sliced into short, thin strips (about 1 1/2 C.)

3 green onions, sliced, or 1 Tbsp. dried chopped onion

1 C. creamy or chunky peanut butter

3/4 C. chopped cilantro, divided use

1/2 C. peanuts or cashews, chopped, for garnish

1. Heat oil in a large stockpot over low heat while dicing chicken breast on a large cutting board with a sharp chef's knife. (It's easier to dice chicken if chicken is partially frozen)

2. Turn heat to high and brown chicken breast in the pot, stirring to avoid burning it, until sides are golden brown, about 5 minutes.

3. Add broth, garlic powder, pineapple juice, and soy sauce.

4. Break noodles into 2-inch lengths and add to pot along with red pepper flakes. Cover with a lid and allow mixture to gently boil 6–7 minutes.

5. While mixture is boiling, slice bell pepper and green onions. When noodles are almost tender, add bell pepper, green onions, peanut butter, and 1/2 C. of the cilantro, stirring until peanut butter is blended into the broth.

6. Turn heat to medium-low and allow mixture to simmer 5 minutes, until bell pepper and noodles are tender.

To serve, sprinkle with peanuts and more cilantro.

Options: You can break up the noodles into smaller lengths before placing them in the soup, or you can twirl them around a fork and slurp them!

RED BEANS AND RICE SOUP

Prep time: 30 minutes | Makes 6 1 1/2-cup servings

This soup was inspired by a chickpea soup I ordered at The Oasis, a downtown Salt Lake City restaurant. The beauty of this soup is that by using frozen onion, frozen green pepper, and bagged spinach, you don't have any peeling and chopping of veggies at all! But you can cut the spinach into smaller ribbons if you prefer.

1 pkg. red beans and rice mix (such as Zatarain's)

6 C. water

1 can red beans, rinsed and drained (1 1/3 C.)

1 1/2 C. jarred or fresh salsa (mild, medium, or hot, your choice)

1 C. chopped ham or chicken

1. Place all ingredients in a 4-quart stockpot.

2. Bring mixture to a boil.

3. Reduce heat to simmer. Cook, stirring occasionally to prevent sticking, until rice is tender, about 20 minutes.

Options: Add slices of sausage, such as kielbasa or andouille, if desired. This soup can also be made in a large, microwavable casserole bowl. Cook, covered, for about 5 minutes on high, until soup starts to come to a boil. Then reduce power to low, cover, and cook an additional 15–20 minutes, or until rice is tender.

TUSCAN BEAN AND KALE SOUP

Prep time: 25 minutes | Makes 6 1 1/2-cup servings

Kale is a good-for-you leafy green that perks up the color in this soup. Frozen mirepoix blend (carrots, celery, and onion) saves time, as does buying the ham already diced. Since the ham is already salty, don't add any extra salt to this soup.

1. Heat oil in a large stockpot. Add mirepoix blend, stirring while cooking, for about 5 minutes over high heat.

2. Add ham, beans, broth, water, seasonings, tomato paste, and kale to pot. Bring to a gentle boil and cook about 10–15 minutes, or until celery and carrots are tender.

3. Taste, and add more seasonings, salt, or pepper if desired. If broth seems a bit salty, add an extra 1/2 C. water.

Option: For a heartier soup, add two C. of frozen diced hash brown potatoes.

1 Tbsp. canola oil

1 12-oz. pkg. frozen mirepoix blend (or 2/3 C. fresh chopped onion, 1/3 C. sliced celery, and 1/3 C. chopped carrots)

2 C. diced ham

2 15-oz. cans cannellini or other white beans, drained and well rinsed (about 2 1/2 C.)

2 14-oz. cans chicken broth (or 3 1/2 C. water and 3 chicken bouillon cubes)

1 C. water

1 Tbsp. garlic powder

1 tsp. dried basil

1/2 tsp. dried thyme

1/2 tsp. dried rosemary

1/2 tsp. oregano (or use 2 1/2 tsp. Italian seasoning)

Pepper to taste

2 Tbsp. tomato paste, optional

3–4 C. chopped kale

CHICKPEA AND SPINACH SOUP

Prep time: 30 minutes | *Makes 6 1 1/2-cup servings*

This soup was inspired by a chickpea soup I ordered at The Oasis, a downtown Salt Lake City restaurant. The beauty of this soup is that by using frozen onion, frozen green pepper, and bagged spinach, you don't have any peeling and chopping of veggies at all! But you can cut the spinach into smaller ribbons if you prefer.

1 Tbsp. olive oil
1 1/2 C. frozen chopped onion (about 1 C. fresh)
1/2 C. frozen green pepper (or about 1/3 C. fresh)
3 14-oz. cans chicken or vegetable broth
1 14.5-oz. can petite-diced tomatoes
2 15.5-oz. cans chickpeas (garbanzo beans) drained, and rinsed
1 bay leaf
1/2 tsp. dried thyme
1 tsp. dried basil
1 Tbsp. garlic powder
1 tsp. sugar
Freshly ground pepper to taste
Salt to taste
4 C. fresh spinach leaves

1. Heat olive oil over medium-high heat in a 4-quart stockpot. Add onion and green pepper, and sauté while stirring for about 10 minutes, until softened.

2. Add broth, tomatoes, chickpeas, bay leaf, thyme, basil, garlic, and sugar. Bring soup to a gentle boil and cook about 10 minutes, until onions and peppers are completely soft and flavors are well blended.

3. While soup is cooking, pack 1 C. of spinach leaves into a larger bowl or cup. With kitchen shears, snip leaves several times into strips. Repeat with all 4 cups of spinach. (Or if desired, leave spinach leaves intact.)

4. Remove soup from heat and stir in spinach leaves. Let soup sit for a few minutes before serving. Add salt and pepper to taste.

Options: If you are not making this as a vegetarian soup, you can add chopped ham or chicken.

SPICY BLACK BEAN SOUP

Prep time: 15 minutes | Makes 6 1-cup servings

This soup draws much of its flavor from chipotle chiles. These smoked jalapeño peppers are found in the Mexican food aisle in seven-ounce cans with adobo sauce. Start with using just one pepper; taste the finished soup, and if you prefer more heat, mince another chile or two and stir it in to the soup. Don't let the rest of the can go to waste; freeze it and then shave off a bit every time you need to add a little kick to a dish. Be sure to drain and rinse your canned beans first. In one recipe test, I tried skipping this step, and the soup was wayyyyy too salty.

3 15-oz. cans black beans, drained and
    rinsed
 2 Tbsp. dried chopped onion
1 14-oz. can vegetable broth, chicken
    broth, or water
1 C. salsa
1 chipotle chile in adobo sauce, with
    1 Tbsp. of the sauce (or more if
    desired) minced
1 7-oz. can green chiles
2 tsp. cumin
2 tsp. garlic powder
1/4 C. chopped cilantro, optional
Salt to taste
Freshly ground pepper to taste
Garnish: Sour cream, chopped
    tomatoes, cilantro, shredded
    cheese, avocado

1. Pour 2 cans of rinsed and drained beans into a blender with onion flakes.

2. Add broth or water and puree until slightly chunky. Pour into a large microwavable casserole bowl (at least 2 1/2 quarts).

3. Add third can of beans to bowl along with salsa, minced chile in adobo sauce, chiles, cumin, garlic, and cilantro.

4. Microwave on high for 10 minutes, until mixture is hot and bubbling. Add pepper or more cumin to taste.

Top each serving with a dollop of sour cream, chopped tomatoes, chopped cilantro, cheese, or avocado slice.

CRUNCHY ALMOND-CELERY SOUP

Prep time: 30 minutes | Makes about 6 1-cup servings

The California Almond Board served an almond chicken soup to journalists covering the National Chicken Cooking Contest in Sacramento in 2001. That sparked my idea for a creamy soup with lots of crunch from both almonds and celery. I broke one of my cardinal rules against using cream-of-something soup! But in this case, it's fairly well disguised.

1. Place chicken broth, onion, and garlic powder in a 4-quart stockpot over medium-high heat.

2. While stock is heating, thinly slice celery and add to pot. Bring to a gentle boil and cook celery for 10 minutes.

3. Stir in chicken soup, milk, almonds, basil, and thyme. Simmer 10–15 more minutes or until celery is tender.

2 Tbsp. olive or canola oil
1 14-oz. can chicken broth
1 C. frozen diced onion (or 3/4 C. fresh; 1/2 of a large onion)
1 tsp. garlic powder
3 C. sliced celery
1 can cream of chicken soup (for a vegetarian soup, use cream of celery)
1 C. milk or half-and-half
1 C. sliced or slivered almonds
1/2 tsp. dried basil
1 tsp. dried thyme
1/2 C. sour cream, optional

HERBED BEAN AND BACON SOUP

Prep time: 25–30 minutes | *Makes about 6 1 1/2-cup servings*

This soup's fragrant, thick broth, which usually comes from hours of slow simmering, gets some help from garlic-flavored croutons. Be sure to rinse the beans thoroughly to remove extra salt.

1 Tbsp. oil
1 C. frozen chopped onion
1 3-oz. pkg. real bacon pieces
1 Tbsp. garlic powder
2 14-oz. cans chicken broth
1 C. water
2 15-oz. cans white beans (Great Northern, navy, or cannellini), drained and rinsed
2 bay leaves
2 tsp. dried rosemary leaves or 2 Tbsp. fresh rosemary leaves
1 tsp. dried basil or 1 Tbsp. fresh chopped basil
1 14.5--oz. can petite-diced tomatoes
1 tsp. lemon juice
2 C. garlic-flavored croutons
Pepper to taste

1. Heat oil in a stockpot over medium-high heat.

2. Add onion and cook about 5 minutes, stirring occasionally.

3. Stir in bacon pieces, garlic powder, broth, water, beans, bay leaves, rosemary, basil, tomatoes, and lemon juice. Bring soup to a gentle boil.

4. Stir in croutons. Turn heat to medium and let soup cook about 10 more minutes, while stirring to help croutons dissolve and thicken soup. If soup seems too thick, thin with 1/2 C. water. Add pepper to taste.

Option: Add a handful of chopped flat-leaf parsley.

SPICY LENTIL AND SAUSAGE STEW

Prep time: 40 minutes | *Makes about 6 1 1/2-cup servings*

Because they're so tiny, lentils cook more quickly than beans and don't need to be presoaked. This recipe is fairly spicy; you can use mild sausage if you don't want as much kick. If you want even more heat, add a few crushed red pepper flakes or a bit of Cajun-style blackened seasoning.

2 C. brown lentils
1 lb. ground hot Italian sausage
2 C. frozen diced onion
1 Tbsp. garlic powder
2 C. frozen chopped green pepper
4 14-oz. cans chicken stock
2 bay leaves
2 14.5-oz. cans petite-diced tomatoes
1/2 C. apple juice
Salt and pepper to taste

1. Set lentils in a strainer or colander and rinse them in hot water. Set aside.

2. In a large pot, over high heat, sauté sausage until browned, about 2–3 minutes.

3. Add onion, garlic, green peppers, and lentils. Cook and stir 2–3 minutes, until onion and peppers are softened.

4. Add chicken stock and bay leaves. Bring soup to a boil then reduce heat to medium.

5. Cook, covered, for 30 minutes at a gentle boil, or until lentils are tender.

6. Add tomatoes and apple juice and cook a few minutes longer.

7. Taste and add salt and pepper if needed.

SLOW COOKER VEGETARIAN LENTIL STEW

Prep time: 5 minutes, Cooking time: 3–4 hours or 6–8 hours | *Makes about 6 1-cup servings*

This meatless meal is full of spicy, sweet flavors. And it's all done in a slow cooker for easy preparation.

1 C. brown lentils
2 14-oz. cans vegetable broth
2 Tbsp. dried onion
1 pkg. frozen mirepoix blend (or 2/3 C. fresh chopped onion, 1/3 C. sliced celery, and 1/3 C. chopped carrots)
1/2 tsp. freshly ground pepper
1 tsp. garlic powder
1 14-oz. can coconut milk
2 Tbsp. curry powder
2 Tbsp. tomato paste
1/2 C. golden raisins

1. Rinse lentils under hot water in sieve or colander.

2. Place broth, lentils, onions, vegetables, pepper, garlic powder, coconut milk, curry powder, tomato paste, and raisins in a slow cooker on high heat. Cook for 3 to 4 hours on high heat, 6 to 8 hours on low. If soup is too thick, thin with vegetable broth or water.

BLACK BEAN AND HAM SOUP

Prep time: 30 minutes | *Makes about 6 1 1/2-cup servings*

This hearty and healthy soup recipe was shared with me by Kirk Shaw, senior editor at Covenant Communications. I streamlined it by using frozen and presliced vegetables. You can buy the ham already cubed as well to make a quick one-pot meal.

In olive oil, sauté onion, bell pepper, carrot, and garlic until tender, about 5 minutes. Add beans and chicken broth and bring to a boil. Reduce heat and add ham, cumin, salt, and pepper. Simmer for 20 minutes. Garnish with sour cream, cilantro, avocado, or cheese.

2 Tbsp. olive oil
2 C. frozen chopped onion (or 1 large fresh onion, chopped)
1 1/2 C. frozen chopped green bell pepper (or 1 large green bell pepper, chopped)
1 C. matchstick-cut or sliced carrots
1 tsp. garlic powder (or about 3 cloves of garlic, minced)
2 (15- oz.) cans black beans
2 14-oz. cans chicken broth
1 1/2 C. cooked ham, cubed
1/2 tsp. cumin
Salt and black pepper to taste
Garnish with any or all: sour cream, cilantro, avocado, cheddar cheese

FIFTEEN-BEAN SOUP

Prep time: 10 hours, Active work time: 15 minutes

It's fun to see the different colors and sizes of beans floating around in this soup. Your slow cooker makes the bean-soaking job simple. Many bean soup mixes come with a packet of seasoning; it's mostly salt and liquid smoke flavoring. If the ham you use is already salty, you may not want to add more salt from the seasoning packet. Add your own liquid smoke if you desire. If you happen to have a ham hock left over from a picnic or holiday ham, add it for more flavor.

1 20-oz. pkg. 12- or 15-bean soup mix
1 12-oz. pkg. mirepoix (or 2/3 C. fresh chopped onion, 1/3 C. sliced celery, and 1/3 C. chopped carrot)
2 8-oz. pkg. of tiny-diced ham (about 2 C.; add a ham hock if you have it)
1 16-oz. jar mild salsa (medium or hot if you desire more heat)
2 Tbsp. dried chopped onion
1 14-oz. can chicken broth
2 C. hot water
1–2 tsp. liquid smoke
1 C. kale or spinach, in ribbons
Several grinds of pepper

1. Place beans in slow cooker and cover with 2 quarts (8 C.) water. Cook on low heat for 6–8 hours (or 3–4 hours on high), until beans are tender.

2. Using hot pads, carefully pour beans into a colander or strainer in the sink. Rinse thoroughly with warm water.

4. Turn the slow cooker to high. Place vegetables, rinsed beans, ham, salsa, onion, broth, water, and liquid smoke in cooker.

5. Cook soup for at least 1 hour on high, 2 hours on low, or until vegetables are tender and flavors have blended.

6. While soup is cooking, slice kale or spinach into thin ribbons. Add to pot 5 minutes before serving. Add pepper to taste.

Tropical Pineapple and Sweet Potato 160

Creamy Pear, Blue Cheese, and Bacon Soup 162

Watermelon Gazpacho 164

Tangy Strawberry Soup 165

Tex-Mex Queso Soup 166

Better Cheddar Soup.. 168

Cheesy Onion Soup 170

FRUIT AND CHEESE SOUPS

TROPICAL PINEAPPLE AND SWEET POTATO

Prep time: 30 minutes | *Makes 6 1 1/2-cup servings*

I've tried a couple of different pineapple-sweet potato and pineapple soups in restaurants. A blustery November day seemed a good time to make up my own version, steaming up my kitchen with tropical flavors. Almost as good as a Caribbean vacation!

1/4 C. dried minced onion
2 14-oz. cans chicken broth or
    vegetable broth
1 24-oz. bag frozen sweet potatoes
    (such as Ore-Ida Steam 'n' Mash),
    or 4–5 C. fresh sweet potatoes,
    peeled and rough-chopped
1 20-oz. can crushed pineapple or
    pineapple tidbits, packed in juice
2 13.5-oz. cans coconut milk
1 Tbsp. pumpkin pie spice (or 1 tsp.
    cinnamon, 1/2 tsp. nutmeg, 1/2
    tsp. ginger, 1/2 tsp. allspice, 1/2
    tsp. cloves)
2 Tbsp. brown sugar
1/2 tsp. pepper, or to taste
1/2 tsp. salt, or to taste

1. Place all ingredients in a 4-quart stockpot over high heat.

2. When soup comes to a gentle boil, reduce heat and simmer for 15 minutes.

3. Remove soup from heat, allow to cool about 5 minutes, and then puree in two or three batches in a stand blender, leaving hole in blender lid open to allow steam to escape.

4. Taste; add more seasonings if desired. Garnish with spices, flaked coconut, or chopped macadamia nuts.

CREAMY PEAR, BLUE CHEESE, AND BACON SOUP

Prep time: 30 minutes | *Makes about 6 1 1/4-cup servings*

My inspiration came from a soup that used pears and blue cheese, served at Salt Lake City's annual Art and Soup fund-raiser by Victor Durrant, chef of Red Rock Junction of Park City. His dish was creamy and mellow but loaded with three sticks of butter, one and a half pounds of cream cheese, and one cup of heavy cream. (No wonder it tasted so good!) The recipe I developed is still pretty rich, even though there's no cream and a lot less cream cheese and butter. I bypassed peeling and slicing pears; canned pears are a practical alternative since the soup is pureed anyway. I added some bacon for a smoky, salty element.

1 Tbsp. butter
1 C. frozen chopped onion
1 29-oz. can pears, packed in juice
1 15-oz. can pears, packed in juice
1 chicken bouillon cube
2 C. water
2 tsp. cinnamon
2 Tbsp. lemon juice
1/4 tsp. pepper
1 tsp. nutmeg
1 3-oz. pkg. crumbled bacon or
   packaged real bacon bits (3/4 C.),
   divided
8 oz. pkg. cream cheese
1 1/2 C. blue cheese crumbles,
   divided

1. Melt butter on in a stockpot over high heat. Add onion and cook, stirring, until softened and translucent.

2. Add pears and their juice, water, cinnamon, lemon juice, pepper, nutmeg, and 1/2 C. of the bacon; simmer on medium-high 10 minutes.

3. Turn off heat; stir in cream cheese and 1 C. blue cheese. Puree with a hand-held immersion blender or in a stand blender, in two batches. If using a stand blender, take care to first start on low speed and then move to high, and leave the middle hole in blender lid open to allow steam to escape.

4. Serve garnished with reserved bacon and blue cheese crumbles.

WATERMELON GAZPACHO

Prep time: 15 minutes | *Makes about 6 1-cup servings*

Americans embraced Spanish gazpacho during the 1960s, when it was quite chic to slurp this ice-cold tomato-based soup. Over the years, people have also added their own twists, including watermelon. In this version, the balsamic vinegar brings out the watermelon's sweetness, and the basil adds an herbal hint. Fresh basil will taste much better in this recipe.

1 medium cucumber, peeled and coarsely diced

1/3 C. red onion, coarsely diced

1/3 C. chopped fresh basil

8–9 C. seedless watermelon, in chunks (about half of a medium-sized watermelon) Or use a regular watermelon and pick out as many seeds as possible

1 Tbsp. balsamic vinegar

1/2 tsp. salt, optional

1. Peel and dice cucumber and onion, place in blender. Add basil.

2. Cut watermelon into chunks, measure, and place in blender.

3. Puree until chunky-smooth. This tastes better ice-cold, so refrigerate until just before serving.

TANGY STRAWBERRY SOUP

Prep time: 10 minutes | Makes about 6 1 1/4-cup servings

This chilled soup makes a nice dessert or first course. If you want a sweeter soup, use strawberry-flavored yogurt instead of plain.

1. Place strawberries in a blender. Add milk and thawed juice concentrate.
2. Blend on high until pureed.

3. Pour into a large bowl and add yogurt and nutmeg, mixing well.

4. Serve chilled in small bowls with a garnish of mint or a fresh berry.

1 16 oz. pkg. frozen strawberries, partially thawed
2 C. milk
1 12-oz. container frozen apple-raspberry fruit juice concentrate (Old Orchard), thawed
2 6-oz. cartons plain yogurt (can be Greek-style)
1/2 tsp. nutmeg

TEX-MEX QUESO SOUP

Prep time: 20 minutes | *Makes about 6 1-cup servings*

A lot of Texans have a special place in their heart for Velveeta, since it's one of just two ingredients needed for making chile con queso dip. Yes, Velveeta's processed and not politically correct, but it melts so nicely with Ro-Tel tomatoes. Here's a spinoff of the classic tortilla chip dip. If you've ever dipped in a few chips and thought, "This tastes so good I could eat it with a spoon"—well, now you can.

1 lb. Velveeta (processed pasteurized cheese product)
2 10-oz. cans tomatoes with chiles (Ro-Tel)
1 7-oz. can mild green chiles
1 1/2 C. milk
Garnishes: Tortilla strips, red pepper strips, cilantro sprigs

1. Cut cheese into cubes and place in a large microwavable bowl.

2. Add tomatoes and green chiles. Microwave, covered, on high for 5 minutes.

3. Stir and return to microwave for 2 more minutes.

4. Stir in milk until mixture is well blended. Microwave 2–3 minutes more to heat through. If soup is too thick, thin with a little milk.

5. Garnish each bowl with tortilla chips.

 Option: You can cook this on the stovetop by mixing the cheese, tomatoes, and chiles in a pot. Cook, stirring, until cheese is melted and mixture is bubbly. Stir in the milk and blend well.

BETTER CHEDDAR SOUP

Prep time: 30 minutes | *Makes about 6 1 1/4-cup servings*

This soup gets a jump-start with frozen mirepoix blend (chopped carrots, celery, and onion). If you can't find this blend in your grocery store, you can use two-thirds cup fresh chopped onion, one-third cup sliced celery, and one-third cup chopped carrot. It will take a little extra time chopping the veggies, but the rest of the soup comes together quickly, especially if you use preshredded cheese.

2 Tbsp. butter
1 12-oz. pkg. frozen mirepoix blend
    (or 2/3 C. fresh chopped onion,
    1/3 C. sliced celery, and 1/3 C.
    chopped carrots)
1 tsp. dried thyme
1 bay leaf
3 Tbsp. flour
2 14-oz. cans chicken or vegetable
    broth (or 4 C. water plus 4
    bouillon cubes)
1 8-oz. pkg. cream cheese, cut into
    chunks
3 C. (12 oz.) shredded extra-sharp
    cheddar cheese
Grinds of pepper to taste

1. Melt the butter in a stockpot over medium-high heat. Add chopped vegetables and cook about 5 minutes, stirring as moisture evaporates (if using frozen veggies).

2. Add thyme, bay leaf, and flour. Stir to evenly blend in flour while mixture cooks for a few minutes.

3. Add broth and bring mixture to a gentle boil, stirring occasionally with a wire whisk to keep vegetables and flour from sticking on bottom of pan, about 5–10 minutes.

4. Meanwhile, cut cream cheese in chunks, and shred cheddar, if necessary.

5. When soup mixture has thickened, turn heat to medium-low and whisk in cream cheese, stirring constantly for about 5 minutes as cream cheese melts. Then remove soup from stove and whisk in cheddar cheese until smooth. Add pepper to taste. Serve as is, or puree in blender for a smooth texture. Garnish with a sprig of thyme.

Options: Add 1–2 C. diced cooked potatoes, bell peppers, broccoli, or other favorite vegetables before adding the cream cheese and cheddar.

CHEESY ONION SOUP

Prep time: 30 minutes │ *Makes about 6 1 1/2-cup servings*

This is a riff on Outback Steakhouse's "Walkabout" cheesy onion soup. Thinly slice the onions so they will caramelize quickly. Velveeta adds to the ease because it melts well and doesn't go grainy. The result is a velvety, rich-flavored broth.

1/4 C. butter
3 large yellow onions, peeled and
    thinly sliced (about 5 C.)
1/4 C. flour
3 14-oz. cans beef broth
1/2 C. milk
12 oz. (3/4 lb.) Velveeta cheese, sliced
    in large chunks
1 tsp. freshly ground pepper
Shredded cheddar cheese and bacon
    bits, for garnish

1. In 4-to-6-quart stockpot, melt butter over low heat while you slice onions. Cut each onion in half down the middle. Pull off outer peel. Place one half of onion, cut side down, on a cutting board and thinly slice. Repeat with other onion half and other two onions.

2. Turn heat to high and cook onion, stirring frequently, about 5 minutes. Turn heat to medium-high and continue cooking another 5 minutes, until onions turn clear.

3. In a cup, mix flour with 1/2 C. of the broth until well blended. Add remaining broth to onion mixture. Whisk in broth/flour mixture so there are no lumps. Allow soup to come to a gentle boil, stirring as soup thickens.

4. Add milk and Velveeta cheese. Simmer about 10 minutes, stirring frequently, until cheese is melted and all ingredients are blended.

5. Serve garnished with shredded cheddar cheese or bacon bits.

TIPS FOR SAVVY SOUP-MAKERS

1. Organize your cupboards and pantry so you know where ingredients are. I've wasted precious minutes rummaging through my cupboards looking for the pasta or a can of beans.

2. Ditto for kitchen equipment. My knives are displayed on a magnetic rack so that they're easy to grab, and so someone won't cut themselves while rifling through my drawers. If several family members also cook, get everyone on the same page as far as where things should go. In fact, Julia Child's Cambridge kitchen had peg-boards with silhouettes drawn of pan sizes so the many people helping out would know which pan belonged where. I've often yearned for some of those peg-boards!

3. Make a weekly general menu plan so you can look ahead, have the right ingredients on hand, put meats in the refrigerator to thaw overnight, and so on.

4. Be flexible enough to punt when you need to. So you're making Salsa Chicken Soup and discover that someone ate all the tortilla chips. Throw a cup of rice into the soup instead.

5. Be judicious about gadgets and equipment. You can chop a stalk of celery in a fraction of the time that it would take to drag a machine out of the cupboard, assemble and disassemble it, and clean all the little parts.

6. Get family members to help. Teens or spouses can perfect a signature recipe so that it becomes their go-to dish. Applaud their specialties.

7. Stock-up on time-saving convenience items when they're on sale, such as canned beans, jarred salsa, or dried minced onion.

8. Invest in a good, sharp chef's knife and a cutting board big enough to hold the food but small enough to fit in the dishwasher. They make the chore of chopping so much easier.

9. Master the art of multitask cooking. Water can be heating to boil while you're chopping vegetables, for instance.

10. Ready-prepped veggies cost more but may be worth it if you actually use them. A huge percentage of fresh produce goes to waste sitting in refrigerators. Comparison shop. Many supermarkets offer precut fresh vegetables, but you can usually save money buying frozen. And for many soups, it's not critical whether it's fresh or frozen.

11. Use leftovers as "planned-overs." If there are meat or veggies at the end of a meal that can be used in tomorrow's soup, dice them up before you store them in the fridge so they are ready to go the next day.

12. The microwave can be put to good use for things besides popping popcorn and heating frozen dinners. Many soups can be quickly cooked in the microwave, and so can rice, potatoes, and other vegetables for soup making. The energy costs are less than cooking on a stovetop.

12. Use fresh vegetables in season when they're cheaper and taste fresher. If you're making tomato soup in the winter, you might as well use canned tomatoes.

13. Add extra veggies if you have them. Chopped bell peppers or celery, and frozen corn or peas add color, flavor, and nutrition.

14. Grow your favorite herbs year-round in your kitchen window. It's convenient to be able to cut a few sprigs as needed, and packets of fresh herbs can cost around two dollars in grocery stores.

15. Yellow onions are often forty cents to fifty cents less per pound than red (purple) onions.

16. Dried beans, per cooked serving, are often less than half the price of canned beans. But they take a lot of time to cook. Soak a batch overnight in your slow cooker on low heat, then portion and freeze for later use. One fifteen-ounce can of rinsed and drained beans is about one and one-third cups.

17. Post a "must use" list on the fridge of leftover items like cooked chicken, or the half-full can of tomato paste so you can incorporate them into meals.

18. Many soups freeze well, but be sure to label them so you don't have mystery containers stuck in the back of the freezer.

19. Serve soups in smaller bowls. Studies show that when people are served on larger plates, they take larger helpings, whether they're really hungry or not. If the first bowl didn't satisfy, they can always go back for seconds.

20. Pack leftover soup for lunch the next day instead of eating out.

21. Soup makes a nice gift for an elderly relative or friend. Most soups are easier to eat than crunchy salads and chewy meats, and they often contain the same valuable nutrients. Every time you make a batch of soup, freeze one portion in a single-serve, microwavable container and label it clearly. Next time you go visiting, you can bring a "care package" of a variety of soups.